A Career Ro
Wildly successful career

WIN AT ➤ WORK

Second Edition

Qiana Williams

Printed in the United States of America

Second Edition

ISBN-13: 9781521126745

Win At Work

168 Pioneer Circle

Pickerington, OH 43147

www.winatwork.net

For permission requests, write to the publisher, addressed "Attention: Permissions
Coordinator," at the address above.

Ordering Information:

Quantity sales. Special discounts are available on quantity purchases by corporations,
associations, and others. For details, contact the publisher at the address above.

Orders by U.S. trade bookstores and wholesalers.

Please contact (614)813-4124.

qiana.williams@gmail.com

To Tyler & Miles,
my inspiration for
everything I do.

I love you more.

"Human beings, individually or collectively cannot transform or uplift themselves without taking full responsibility for doing so. This is a law of nature. Once full responsibility is accepted others can assist as long as it is understood that they cannot be responsible. No group in history has been lifted into excellence or competitiveness by another group."

Shelby Steele

CONTENTS

WIN
AT WORK

OH, THE PLACES YOU'LL GO!

"If at first you don't succeed,
Dust yourself off, and try again
You can dust it off and try again, try again."
- Aaliyah, Try Again

It was the Fall of 1995. I had just graduated from college. I was the living embodiment of the Dr. Seuss book, Oh, The Places You'll Go.

"Congratulations!
Today is your day.
You're off to Great Places!
You're off and away!"

I had my degree in hand and I was officially on the job market. I was brimming with hope. The world was my oyster. I had visions of power suits, business lunches and a corner office with a view. This was my time.

"You have brains in your head. You have feet in your shoes. You can steer yourself any direction you choose. You're on your own. And you know what you know. And YOU are the one who'll decide where to go..."

Even when I got my tenth rejection letter, I wasn't daunted. Confused? Yes. But, daunted. Nope. Not even a little bit. I mean I had my degree. Of course, I was going to find a job. It was taking a little bit longer than I anticipated, yes, but I still expected that any day the call would come from my dream employer, offering me the dream job, with the right number of zeros behind the offer and then I would be on my way to the land of power lunches, rubbing elbows with movers and shakers. It was all just a matter of time. I was going to make my mark on the world. I was unbothered by what felt like a temporary delay.

Now mind you my plan A, become a probation officer had went up in smoke (After several eye-opening interviews, I realized I wasn't cut out for that life.) And, even though I didn't have a Plan B or even a Plan Z for that matter. I had my degree. That was the key, right? That's what I had been told my whole life. Get your degree. Then you'll get a great job. You'll work really hard. Climb the ladder. Make great money. Become the youngest Vice President in the company's history. You'll be a success.

"KID, YOU'LL MOVE MOUNTAINS!

So...
be your name Buxbaum or Bixby or Bray
or Mordecai Ali Van Allen O'Shea,
you're off to Great Places!
Today is your day!
Your mountain is waiting.
So...get on your way!"

I kept applying for jobs and going on the occasional job interview, but six months after graduation nothing had panned out and I needed an income. Ok. Now, I was officially starting to panic. So, I mustered what little hope I had left and I signed up with a temp agency. This was not the life I had envisioned. To add insult to injury, it seemed like every day I got a phone call or email about someone else who graduated with me who had just landed an amazing gig. People all around me living the life I had dreamed of, all while I sat staring blankly at computer screen behind a reception desk, answering phones and welcoming visitors who had come to meet with the bigwigs in the corner office. The corner office I was supposed to be sitting in with my brand new degree hanging on the wall.

"When you're in a Slump,
you're not in for much fun.
Un-slumping yourself
is not easily done."

As sad as this story was, and believe me having a front row seat in your own personal career melodrama was pretty pitiful. Still, I was not a victim. It is true that nothing went the way I thought it should have. It is also true that there were people all around me, people who went to the same stellar university and had the same Liberal Arts degree who were faring exponentially better than I was. Did they have some magic potion? Nope. Did they have a trust fund? Maybe, but that wasn't the difference. The difference was they had a plan and I didn't.

I had a degree. They had worked summer internships or co-ops. They had cultivated networks and relationships. Which in turn meant they had people to call to get interview "hook-ups" or to find out about jobs. I had none of that. While I had spent the last four years with my head down in my books, working random part-time retail jobs, they understood that attending college and securing their degree was important, but only one part of the equation. They understood that to be successful you had to plan for life after college versus my approach of merely expecting that my degree alone would open doors.

"Out there things can happen, and frequently do,
To people as brainy and footsy as you.
And when things start to happen, don't worry, don't stew.
Just go right along, you'll start happening too!"

No one ever told me I needed a plan. Everyone told me I needed a degree. Even when I would sit in class and I would hear the kids around me talk about their internships or co-ops I wouldn't think anything of it. I mean it sounded cool, but it didn't sound like it was necessary. They were interning at Proctor & Gamble. I was working at FootAction. We were all working, right? Yes and no. My aspirations weren't a career in retail. So, logging 20-30 hours a week helping teenagers try on shoes wasn't the same as a Business major helping plan and execute marketing campaigns while spending the Summer working in the Marketing department at a marketing powerhouse like P&G.

So be clear. What no one told me, I'm telling you. You need a plan. You need a roadmap. A guide that will get you from point A to point B. No matter what stage you are in in your career you need a roadmap. And, that's what you're holding in your hand. So, whether you're a new college graduate or someone looking to change companies or careers. Or maybe you're just ready to get promoted. This book was written with you in mind. Every single word.

There are times when the toughest part of planning is just figuring out where to start. Preparing for a successful career is no different. While it marks a major turning point in your life it doesn't have to be intimidating. Building a successful career, as with any other major life experience you have faced, is all about knowing where you want to go and having a plan to get you there. That's just what the book you're holding in your hands is...a roadmap to help you fulfill your goals and dreams.

So, where do you begin? Well, it might sound strange, but you should begin at the end. I know it sounds cliché, but you must know where you're going to figure out how to get there. Your job is to first create the vision then determine the steps that will get you to your destination. Along the way, you will gather data from failure and success in your own personal life experiences, through trial and error, from observing and taking note of the life experiences of those around you and in a variety of other ways. You will meet and talk to people who have traveled a similar path. You'll learn from their failures and their successes, but remember their path won't be your path. So, although it's key to use others as a resource, you must remember that no two people will have the exact same experience. Your path is your own.

"Just never forget to be dexterous and deft.
And never mix up your right foot with your left.
And will you succeed?
Yes! You will, indeed!
(98 and 3/4 percent guaranteed.)"
    — **Dr. Seuss, Oh, The Places You'll Go!**

Now, let's get busy blazing your trail!

Mantra to Master

"Know who you are and who lives within you, and moving mountains will seem small compared to what you can do."

Marianne Williamson,
A Year of Miracles

THIS IS YOUR EXIT

"There is no greater gift you can give or receive than to honor your calling."
- Ralph Waldo Emerson

Some careers are like cars stuck in rush hour traffic.
Slowly inching along.
Going nowhere.

Does this sound like your career, an unpredictable series of unforeseen starts and stops? Just when things seem to finally be moving along, something unknown to you, happens several cars ahead of you. You veer, you slam on your brakes, your tires make that awful screeching noise and, with all the usual ceremony of a driver swerving to avoid hitting the car in front of them, you come to a dead stop. Of course, you are glad you didn't hit the car in front of you that would have been disastrous. Still, you are rattled. You feel your heart beating double time. Your mind is racing trying to figure out what happened. You were hopeful that was your opportunity. You were sure that was your big chance. You could see the clearing ahead. You were so close to your destination. Now, you're not sure if or when you will be able to move again.

Or maybe your career is more like the driver who jumps from lane to lane trying to get ahead. You finally find your way into the fast lane but, just when you are ready to step on the gas and open it up, the lane slows to a complete stop. You look to your right only to see the car that was behind you five miles ago zooming by.

Maybe you are more like the driver on the side of the road having to fix a blow out in your tire. Not only are you watching as other cars pass by, but you are so out of your element that you can't even begin to think about when you'll be able to get back on the road. The effects of these frustrations are enough to make you throw your hands in the air, leaving the course of your career to the alignment of the sun, moon, and stars.

SURVIVAL OF
THE FITTEST

"Do or do not. There is no try."
– Yoda

Despite what you may have faced or what you might be feeling, the aforementioned experiences don't have to be your reality. Work doesn't have to be frustrating. The power and importance of work has been extolled by some of our greatest thinkers:

"Whoever works his land will have plenty of bread, but he who follows worthless pursuits lacks sense."
– The Bible, Proverbs 12:11

"Choose a job you love, and you will never have to work a day in your life."

- Confucius

"Pleasure in the job puts perfection in the work."
– Aristotle

"The worker must work for the glory of his handiwork, not simply for pay; the thinker must think for truth, not for fame."
- W.E.B. Du Bois

We need to work. Work allows us to take care of our most basic needs. It allows us to put food on the table, support our families, and pay our bills. Once we check these off the list we have other needs that are also critical such as the desire to work for an organization that empowers us, supports our values, provides us with opportunities to develop, acknowledges and rewards our accomplishments, and gives us the space to make a meaningful contribution.

In these ways, work, unlike any other activity, allows for the actualization and fulfillment of the full range of needs as articulated by Maslow in his Hierarchy of Needs. In a nutshell, Maslow believed that we are all motivated to achieve certain needs. When one need is fulfilled we seek to fulfill the next one, and so on and so on. The hierarchy is best thought of as a pyramid, where the lowest levels of the pyramid are made up of our most basic needs and the more complex needs (self-actualization, personal growth, fulfillment of potential) are located at the top of the pyramid. This is why work and the way we engage it is so important. Work provides us with the income to support ourselves and our loved ones, the personal satisfaction of a job well done, the opportunity to be creative, compensation, recognition of our talents and natural abilities, and a sense of belonging to some larger community of individuals who are committed to accomplishing these same goals. Through meaningful work we directly and indirectly realize the fulfillment of many of our hopes and dreams.

This idea is astutely illustrated by Jim Collins in his bestselling book, *Good to Great: Why Some Companies Make the Leap... and Others Don't*: "When [what you are deeply passionate about, what you can be best at in the world, and what drives your economic engine] come together, not only does your work move toward greatness, but so does your life. For, in the end, it is impossible to have a great life unless it is a meaningful life. And it is very difficult to have a meaningful life without meaningful work. Perhaps, then, you might gain that rare tranquility that comes from knowing that you've had a hand in creating something of intrinsic excellence that makes a contribution. Indeed, you might even gain that deepest of all satisfactions: knowing that your short time here on this earth has been well spent, and that it mattered."

By picking up this book you have taken the first step on that journey. This is your roadmap, designed specifically to increase your career savvy and help you access the success you long for to live the life you want. The ideas, strategies, and language used in this book have been shaped by working with many individuals as they seek opportunities in both the public and private sector, in corporate and nonprofit organizations. This is your blueprint to move your thinking from unintentional, hit or miss shots in the dark, to clear, thoughtful, and targeted strategies.

This book is designed to provide you with practical, easy-to-implement strategies that are neither overly complex nor unnecessarily simplistic. While no one resource can have all the answers, *What You Don't Know Can Derail You* is a resource to provide you with the knowledge, information, and, more importantly, rules that have been tested and proven to help you hit the ground running as you work to achieve your career goals.

Anyone who has held a job in the last 10-15 years understands that the way work is structured and how success is defined continues to evolve in significant ways. As such, the rules for becoming successful have also changed. This book is designed to help you understand and apply today's rules. Knowledge of these rules will not only help you understand how the world of work has changed but it will also help you alter the way you need to think and act to have the success you desire.

No matter what your career aspirations are or what level you are in your company, this book can help you develop the strategies to understand the culture, competencies, and strategic behaviors of the company in which you work. With that new understanding and the tools in your toolkit you will be able to transform your thinking enabling you to get a new job, start a new job successfully, get promoted, take on a stretch assignment and/or be identified as a high-potential employee. This, in turn, will aid in increasing your job prospects, developmental opportunities, promotional assignments, and overall earning potential.

HELP ME, HELP YOU.
HELP ME, HELP YOU.
"Stay ready so you don't have to get ready."
- Will Smith

One of my favorite movies is *Jerry Maguire* with Tom Cruise and Cuba Gooding, Jr. I love this movie because, in a very unassuming way, the movie tells a powerful story about work and our responsibility for creating and defining the work we choose to engage in. For those who have never seen the movie here is a brief synopsis: Jerry Maguire (Tom Cruise), a slick, high-living sports agent, has a troubling encounter with the son of an injured athlete he represents. This leads to a serious crisis of conscience when he determines he is tired of the shallowness of his profession and wants to live a more fulfilling, ethical life. During a sleepless night, Jerry writes a memo calling on himself and his colleagues to think more about the long-term welfare of the clients they represent and less about immediate profits. While everyone around him applauds the sentiment, Jerry's superiors think his ideas are bad for business; Jerry is subsequently fired, and, rather than standing in solidarity with him, his "friends" in the firm scramble like sharks to claim Jerry's clients. Jerry finds himself left with one ally, one client and a long road ahead of him. At the end of his last day, the only people willing to join Jerry as he strikes out on his own are staff accountant Dorothy (Renee Zellweger), a single mother secretly in love with Jerry, and Rod Tidwell (Cuba Gooding, Jr.), a football player whose pride and arrogance have gotten in the way of him reaching his full potential.

With all of Jerry's clients gone, he must refocus his priorities. Similarly, Rod, failing to live up to his full potential, is on the verge of being "out of the game" much sooner than he ever anticipated. Both men are forced to answer some hard questions about their careers and about who they are in order to fully realize their hopes and dreams.

While many people remember lines like, "Show me the money," or, "You had me at hello," I think the best line in the movie is, "Help me, help you. Help me, help you." All too often, I see countless examples of people who want the easy path, the path they believe to be of least resistance, the path, to be frank, that requires the least amount of work. And, how ironic is that, right? To expect success to be without some meaningful effort? To those who still believe in the myth of an easy route, I say, for every person you can show me who became successful by the luck of the draw, I'll show you ten who put in work, hard work: Oprah Winfrey, Bill Gates, Condoleezza Rice, Peyton Manning, Michael Jordan, Madame CJ Walker, Steve Jobs, Martin Luther King, Jr., Harriet Tubman, and Leroy Powell, Sr. (that's my grandfather).

So, a caveat to the faint of heart, there are no shortcuts. In these pages, you'll find a proven formula for success. But, this, most assuredly, will require effort. Everything you will learn in these pages, everything you will be asked to do will propel you forward. You will learn important concepts and practice critical skills. You will have to be fully engaged. Most importantly you will have to invest time, effort, and energy. The good news is that the investment is in you and with your new level of focus comes a reward. While there are no guarantees in life, I can assure you that your odds are significantly better applying when a strategic approach than they ever were when you were employing an accidental process, with one eye open and your fingers crossed.

Here is the formula:

knowledge, skills and abilities
(you have/can develop this)

+

the rules
(you need this)

= **Extraordinary Success!**
(let's go get this!)

WHY I WROTE
THIS BOOK

"You are braver than you believe, stronger than you seem, and smarter than you think." - Winnie the Pooh

After my early career fumbles, right out of college, I got my act together. I turned those temp gigs into a full-time job and started creating experiences that would build my resume. Even though I felt like I was behind my peers who had landed positions right out of school, I was confident that I would make up ground quickly. Little did I know, there were still some big lessons ahead of me.

I had just started a new job. I was excited for the new opportunity that was awaiting me. I was also a little nervous. Much of my professional experience and success, to that point, had been built in nonprofit organizations. Now I was heading to the private sector to work for a major fashion retailer. I was exchanging social justice advocacy for bras, panties, lotions and potions. It's an understatement to say I was moving into a very different world. Missions aside, the pace and culture alone were foreign to me. My colleagues seemed to speak a different language, people talked in acronyms and each conversation felt like everyone had read the same Harvard Business Review article, but they'd forgotten to share it with me. I felt like a fish out of water.

The first few months were a struggle. I was making what I believed were simple mistakes, but the environment seemed unforgiving. I felt like I was under a microscope and any minute the jig would be up. I was frustrated, stressed, and overwhelmed. There were many nights I went home completely perplexed and dispirited. I knew I was a hard worker. I was well-educated, driven, and capable. Yet somehow that went right out the window whenever I walked through the company doors. I was so unnerved I began to question my own talents and abilities. Maybe I wasn't as good as I thought. Maybe I was in over my head. My confidence was in the gutter.

The problem was my pride wouldn't let me throw in the towel. One day it was as if I woke out of a coma. I decided this was not going to be my experience anymore. I had excelled in every job I had ever held and I was determined that this job was going to be no different. I approached a manager, Don, who I felt I could trust and I told him what I was experiencing. I asked him, scratch that, I pleaded with him to help me figure out what I was missing. I told him to give it to me straight. He replied, "You have everything you need to be successful. What you need to do is step back and learn the culture here. Look at who is successful and study them. Once you do that you're going to be just fine."

I immediately took his advice. When I say immediately, I mean immediately. I didn't spend time questioning if his advice was accurate or try to convince him that the issue was the environment, my manager, or something else I could not fix. I did not tell him about all the ways the company needed to adjust. Nope. I approached his advice as if it were the gospel, the Holy Grail. Boy, was he right.

You know what happened? In just over four years I received three promotions and increased my salary by more than $30,000. It wasn't easy; there were certainly moments of frustration but, by employing the «rules» outlined here, I've been able to find career success at almost every turn. (It also did not hurt that one morning the Executive Vice President of Human Resources stopped at my desk and said he noticed that I was always there before anyone else, including him. Then he told me to keep up the good work.)

Before we dive into the rules, let's look at this new landscape and three people, each attempting to navigate today's evolving work environment.

Mantra to Master

"Look closely
at the present you are
constructing
it should look like the
future you are dreaming."

Alice Walker

THE NEW WORLD OF WORK

"...Nevertheless, the inescapable reality is that ours is a society based on economic autonomy. Those who are not equipped with the knowledge and skills necessary to get and keep, good jobs are denied full social inclusion and tend to drop out of the mainstream culture, polity, and economy."
- Anthony Carnevale & Donna Derochers, Standards for what? The economic root of K-16 reform

Starting with the Civil War and continuing until the 1970s the United States had been the world's most successful mass-production economy, the very best at producing standardized goods and services at the least cost and selling them at the lowest price. This led to a mass production workforce rivaled by none. The American dream of starting at the bottom and, without much formal education, rising to the top was born out of this system. The United States' dominance rested on a solid agricultural and manufacturing base wherein workers with a high-school education or less could provide a comfortable living for their families. Initial attempts by European and Asian countries to compete with the United States after the post-World War II economic recovery failed because these countries did not have the domestic markets big enough to replicate the United States' strategy of mass production.

Instead, what these countries did was refocus their efforts around building flexible work systems that would allow them to produce more variety as well as emphasize quality. This forced these countries to locate more authority down the line in the hands of skilled workers, thus allowing quality to exist in the production system itself.

While this phenomenon was occurring outside the U.S., within its borders, increased wealth and a growing, restless, and mobile middle class were having its corresponding effects on the United States economy. A

Industrial Economy
• Steady & predictable
• Slow & linear
• Long product lifecycles
• Local competition
• Bigger is better
• Emphasis on stability
• Mass production
• In short supply = Financial capital
• Top down leadership
• Semi-skilled or unskilled workforce
• Innovation occurs at the top
• Hierarchical

growing dissatisfaction with mass-produced goods and services led Americans to start "trading up," spending more for well-designed, well-engineered, and well-crafted goods. This brought about new competitive standards such as quality, variety, customization, convenience, customer service, speed, and novelty. Subsequently, foreign competition was introduced, changing the very nature of what competition looked like and giving birth to a knowledge economy.

The knowledge economy is an age defined by global competition, rampant change, faster flow of information and communication, increasing business complexity, and pervasive globalization. To meet new competitive requirements, businesses have been forced to invest in new, flexible technologies and organizational systems that require fewer but more highly skilled employees.

Knowledge Economy
• **L**ean production – Doing more with less
• In short supply = Human capital
• Shared leadership; self-direction
• Skilled workforce
• Innovation occurs across the enterprise
• Flat organization structures
• Marked by fast change
• Fast & unpredictable
• Short product life spans
• Global competition
• Faster is better
• Change & the ability to manage change

Companies must operate in ways drastically different than before. Because competition is now coming from many different directions, companies must develop and employ processes that allow for innovation, speed, and flexibility. You may be saying to yourself, *"That doesn't sound like anything new. Companies have always tried to beat their competition by gaining market share."* This is vastly different and here is how: competitive advantage was formerly driven by access to raw materials, cheap labor, and cost reduction through economies of scale; in the new economy, competitive advantage is defined by knowledge, processes, and systems. See, markets have opened, technology has advanced, and new economic policies have been created that have changed who plays the game and where the game is played.

As Daniel Pink notes in his groundbreaking book, *A Whole New Mind: Why Right-Brainers Will Rule the Future*, "We are moving from an economy and a society built on the logical, linear, computer like capabilities of the Information Age to an economy and a society built on the inventive, empathic, big-picture capabilities of what's rising in its place, the Conceptual Age."

Creative Economy
• Outsourcing; off-shoring   • Increased globalization   • Abundance   • High touch   • High concept   • Quest for meaning   • Design

Competition from foreign markets has grown to levels that companies in the United States never imagined would occur and thus were unprepared for. In addition to these vast changes more experts are citing a move beyond the Knowledge Economy into what is being referred to as the Creative Economy, an age marked by three main forces: outsourcing, increased globalization, and a quest for meaning driven by increased levels of material abundance.

Much has been made in the news regarding the increasing number of jobs that are moving offshore. But, for the most part, our society has not responded to this phenomenon. Why? Because many the jobs were believed to be low and unskilled work. However, the times are slowly changing. One need only look at the fluctuations happening in Asia to see that the professional lives of workers in the Western world are bound to change. Take, for instance, the growing number of skilled workers being produced by the education system in many developing countries. Or the ease with which the world communicates globally. Now, add to this the fact that it costs significantly less to pay workers who work overseas. One need only to think of all the jobs that could effectively be performed in these low-cost overseas environments. So, what's at risk? Those routine types of jobs that can be reduced to a set of rules, routines, and instructions. Add to this the growing trend toward making processes or machines self-acting. Think TurboTax or CompleteCase.com, where you can get an uncontested divorce for $249, less than a 10th of the cost of a divorce lawyer.

These changes are having a sharp impact on companies and on the way individuals work within them. Companies must create high-performance work systems that drive down the broader responsibilities and general skills required at the points of production and service delivery, allowing workers to get as close to customers as possible. Companies need employees who are prepared to respond to these new demands. The problem is that more companies are reporting that they don't have the talent to fully execute in more senior and organizationally-critical roles.

Any corporate executive will tell you that a strategic focus on talent management is the single most effective thing organizations can do to build a bench of high-quality leaders, capable of executing on future organizational strategy. Organizations that successfully identify and develop high-potential talent will enjoy direct financial performance advantages over their peers. To better understand why organizations have turned their focus to talent we must understand the pressures companies face that make talent the true differentiator.

In their book, *The War for Talent*, Ed Michaels, Helen Handfield-Jones, and Beth Axelrod recount a story that illustrates this dilemma, told to them by Les Wexner, Founder & Chairman of L Brands, formerly Limited Brands.

"In the early 1990s, Limited Brands suffered a tremendous blow. Its earnings took a beating and its stock took a nosedive. Despite his best efforts, Wexner couldn't turn things around. Daunted and frustrated, Wexner decided to reach out to some friends he respected. He sought advice from world renowned director Steven Spielberg, GE's Jack Welch and Wayne Callaway, then CEO of PepsiCo. to determine how they ran their businesses so well.

"I asked them how often they checked sales," Wexner recalls. "They said, 'Once or twice a month.' I checked ours twice a day. I asked them how much time they spent reviewing new ads. They said, 'Almost no time.' I asked them how much time they spent on new product concepts. They said, 'Occasionally—but only on a really big new product concept with a large capital expenditure.' I was spending half my time on products and ads."

Wexner was amazed. Finally, he said, "Well, what do you do?" Separately, each of the men explained that they spent about half their time on people: recruiting new talent, picking the right people for particular positions, grooming young stars, developing global managers, dealing with underperformers, and reviewing the entire talent pool. Welch said to Wexner, "Having the most talented people in each of our businesses is the most important thing. If we don't, we lose."

Wexner returned to his corporate headquarters in Columbus, Ohio and immediately set about implementing these newly-acquired insights. He shifted his product focused lens to a talent mindset. He hired a new right hand to help him design a talent focused blueprint. Together they designed and led a process that reviewed each division's talent strategies and the performance of the top 50 people in each division. He also began to infuse new talent into the organization, hiring top leaders from world-class companies inside and outside the retail industry. The best internals got promoted and those who couldn't cut it were moved aside. In three years, more than half of the people in the top 250 positions were changed. But that was only part of the story.

Also within those three years, the company's performance had significantly improved. Profits had grown from $285 million to $445 million and the company's stock price nearly doubled. The portfolio was reshaped and the merchandising process was fundamentally redesigned. However, ask Wexner and he's crystal clear on what made the difference, "Talent was the most important thing. Without better talent, most of the other actions would not have happened successfully."

If the testimonial of a successful billionaire isn't enough to make you a believer, maybe research from the Corporate Executive Board (CEB) will. CEB is a best practice insight and technology company that works with top companies to share, analyze, and apply proven practices. In a research volume, *Creating Talent Champions*, the CEB further illustrates the point. Most business leaders surveyed in this research reported spending more than 20 hours per week investing in talent-related issues. Despite this significant investment these same leaders reported significant talent gaps. More than half of business leaders said their existing staff lacked critical skills and competencies. However, by far, the biggest issue these leaders reported, was that four in five leaders feel they do not have the people they need for their business to succeed.

This deviation from a strategy primarily focused on goods & services to a strategic focus on talent resulted in a profound shift for the workforce. Just as some companies were unprepared for this transition, certain segments of the workforce were also slow to react. This lack of preparation was exacerbated by several phenomena. Technological advances were rendering some industries obsolete; industries where at one time an individual could make a middle-class income by making widgets all day were no longer willing or able to pay top dollar for these types of jobs; unprepared workers suffered. The United States education system was failing to prepare its students to not only operate, but also compete in the new environment. Once again, certain groups of workers were vulnerable and subsequently suffered.

This opened the door to an influx of foreign-born talent and increased unemployment for a large segment of the United States' workforce who had previously operated in a semi-skilled/unskilled vacuum. This is why we consistently hear about a war for talent despite high unemployment rates. There are, indeed, many bodies, but those individuals don't have the necessary skills or credentials companies are looking for. For better or worse companies are more often looking for ready now talent because they rarely distort resources to invest in the type of on the job /apprentice training of the past. This makes it difficult for low skilled or unskilled workers to gain access to those jobs without some form of college level education or certification.

To solve this problem, workers must understand the new market forces that create value. They must be able to envision and employ the systems and processes that create organizational advantage. That organizational advantage is achieved through those new competitive standards we mentioned earlier. The critical point to understand here is this: the ways in which companies must set themselves apart from their competition, to create a competitive advantage, are now directly tied to the knowledge and skills of their employees. This is great news for the engaged and driven worker.

Today's competitive requirements are based on the need to respond to consumers' desire to make emotional connections and feel good about themselves. They must also address the consumers' need to find help, support, and sometimes escape from their increasingly busy lives. Think Starbucks. People can get coffee anywhere, right? Yet, for some reason they are willing to consistently pay $5 for a cup of joe. Why? The team at Starbucks will tell you why. This is no ordinary cup of coffee, it is superior. Not only are you buying that superior cup of coffee, you are also buying an experience. When you buy a Skinny Latte you're not just buying the drink, you're buying the Italian coffeehouse experience that founder Howard Schultz found so captivating when he first decided to start the company, after a trip to Italy. You are buying the highest quality coffee beans that are, of course, ethically sourced, ensuring you feel good about your contribution to society with every sip. You're buying status. When people see you holding that white cup with green etching and the recycled brown paper sleeve, it sends a certain message about who you are.

Now think about Starbucks in the context of those competitive standards we discussed: excellence, ease, newness, choice, speed to market. Starbucks creates an emotional connection, it offers the highest quality coffee, it boasts a diverse array of drinks, you get it quick, those cute little baristas write your name on your cup, and just about every shop feels like a small community with people gathered around tables talking, reading, working on laptops or, yeah, sipping coffee. Starbucks is a great illustration of a company responding to these growing consumer demands. To be successful, today's companies must, like Starbucks, employ competitive requirements that allow them to respond to and create products and services that tackle these wants and needs.

These market forces are so critical because they are the heart of how today's companies must operate. These competitive requirements cut across industries. Once you understand them, you then need to understand how they apply to your company and the industry you're in to align them to the work you do.

Let's look at each competitive requirement in more detail:

Smart Investment: Simply cutting costs as a means to respond to downturns no longer works. Today's successful companies must balance frugality with the need to invest in the future. This ensures that companies have the technology, talent, and resources to be productive and to successfully compete in the market.

Choice: Remember when Baskin Robbins had only 31 flavors? Now there are more than 50. The ice cream business isn't the only industry that has had to evolve because of increased competition. When you factor in globalization, which is no longer a rarity but is how we do business these days, you can see why having choice is key in achieving success.

Excellence: How often do you like to give your hard-earned money to someone and get a shoddy or subpar product in return? Never, right? Because of the variety of choices available, consumers can and do demand excellence in the products and services they buy.

Ease: Most of us are running in a million directions. Our work days are packed with meetings and our evenings are spent running our children to various events and social activities. What we need in the products and services we use is ease. We need products and services that understand how busy we are and we want to do business with companies that make getting those products and services easy.

Newness: Newness is all about consumers' desire to be on the cutting edge, to have something that no one else does. Think of the spectacle caused by the new Jordan's. Every year or so a new pair of Air Jordan's is released and, as we know, frenzy and sheer delight ensue. Kids from nine to 39 clamor to get a pair. Of course, this isn't limited to tennis shoes. Just ask Apple, Inc.

Speed to market: It's a no-brainer that the first to market with a product or service wins.

While these concepts may seem relatively simple, it's not enough to know that choice is important, but making sense of choice within the context of your company's strategy is pivotal. For example, if you work in an ice cream shop it isn't enough to invent new flavors. What's important is to identify new flavors based on customer data such as sales, surveying customers who shop at your business regularly, looking at industry trends, etc., to make an educated suggestion about what new flavors are going to be successful for your company. As Simon Sinek writes in *Start with Why: How Great Leaders Inspire Everyone to Take Action,* "Put bluntly, the struggle that so many companies have to differentiate or communicate their true value to the outside world is not a business problem, it's a biology problem. And just like a person struggling to put her emotions into words, we rely on metaphors, imagery and analogies to communicate how we feel. Absent the proper language to share our deep emotions, our purpose, cause or belief, we tell stories. We use symbols. We create tangible things for those who believe what we believe to point to and say, "That's why I'm inspired." If done properly, that's what marketing, branding and products and services become; a way for organizations to communicate to the outside world. Communicate clearly and you shall be understood."

How different is this line of thinking from your current mindset? What shifts will this require you to take as you think about your career?

What is the biggest learning you took from this chapter?

Life in the Real World

Understanding Competitive Standards: Mattel

Between 2001 and 2004, Mattel lost 20% of its share of the worldwide fashion-doll segment to smaller rivals such as MGA Entertainment, creator of a hip new line of dolls called Bratz. MGA recognized what Mattel failed to – that preteen girls were becoming more sophisticated and maturing more quickly. At younger ages, they were outgrowing Barbie and increasingly preferring dolls that looked like their teenage siblings and the pop stars they idolized. As the target market for Barbie narrowed from girls age three to 11 to girls about three to five, the Bratz line cut rapidly into the seemingly unassailable Mattel franchise. Mattel finally moved to rescue Barbie's declining fortunes, launching a brand extension called My Scene that targeted older girls, and a line of hip dolls called Flavas to compete head-on with Bratz. But the damage was done. Barbie, queen of dolls for over 40 years, lost a fifth of her realm almost overnight – and Mattel didn't see it coming.

Excerpted from, *Scanning the Periphery*,
Harvard Business Review. November 2005.

Select one of the competitive standards. Identify at least 5 innovative ways for your organization to respond to the selected standard.

Discuss in detail the concept of competitive standards and how they apply in the real-life example on the previous page. What competitive standards did Mattel fail to understand?

Notes:

Now, that you understand the world with which we must all operate, let's look at our three workers.

THE WORKERS

NICOLE
Sales executive who is starting a new job with a new company after 13 years with her last employer.

Nicole has been working for the same company for the last 13 years. She started with the financial institution while pursuing her undergraduate degree and has moved up the ranks quite successfully. Though she has earned several promotions during her tenure she has decided it's time to make a career change. There have been several changes in her department since the financial institution has gone through a major reorganization as the result of a corporate takeover. All of this change has left Nicole feeling unsure of her career prospects with her current employer. So, despite her tenure and seniority with her company, Nicole decides to begin a passive job search. When she sees something of interest she applies, but because she is unsure of what she wants to do next with her career she isn't looking very aggressively.

Nicole happens to run into a friend who mentions to her that a major pharmaceutical company is having an open house hiring event. Not one to pass up a potential opportunity, Nicole decides to attend the event to see what types of opportunities she might find. She meets with a recruiter and has a very nice conversation. About a week later she receives a call from the recruiter inviting her to come back about talk about opportunity position within the training department. Needless to say, Nicole's interest is piqued. She has been facilitating training for the financial institution for the last five years and, though she wasn't originally looking for a training opportunity, she decides it won't hurt to explore. After Nicole's interview things start moving quickly. The pharmaceutical firm extends her an offer making $11,000 more than her current salary. Nicole is sure this is an offer she can't turn down.

She is newly married and she and her husband want to buy a house and have children; not to mention she and her new husband enjoy traveling. A salary increase of this magnitude will really support the lifestyle they want to lead. She discusses the proposition with her husband, they decide it is a good offer, and Nicole accepts. She takes a week off between leaving the financial institution and starting with the pharmaceutical company.

When she arrives at the pharmaceutical company on her first day for orientation, she is given her schedule for the next nine weeks. She has been scheduled to complete an intensive six-week training program, where she will learn the content of the training that she will be responsible for. She will then participate in a two-week train the trainer session and by her ninth week she will be on her own. At that point, she will be responsible for knowing the content and delivering it to a classroom of trainees throughout the company's global footprint.

I had dinner with Nicole two weeks before she was scheduled to be on her own and asked her how her new job was going. She told me the company was a great place to work but the expectations were unreasonable. She complained that it was unrealistic for her to learn the material and be ready to deliver the training in the timeframe they had laid out for her. She had been hired to facilitate training on a software platform known as SAP. She had never utilized SAP before and felt like she shouldn't be expected to grasp the material in only eight week's time.

PETER

Generally, the smartest guy in the room. Struggling to adapt to the style of his new manager. His frustrations may put his ability to keep his dream job in jeopardy.

Peter grew up in a working-class neighborhood. Peter's mother and father are both teachers. He has two Master's degrees and is currently pursuing a doctoral degree. All his life experiences to this point have given Peter an intimate understanding of the challenges students face in the classroom. Peter's schooling has also allowed him to become thoroughly familiar with most theories in the field of education. As such, he has developed very definitive opinions and views about what does and doesn't work in education. Because Peter has spent so much time studying the problem he is viewed as, and believes himself to be, an expert on Urban Education. Peter believes solving the American education crisis is key to solving the issues plaguing poor and low-income communities. His passion for the subject is evident.

Peter has spent most of his life in a university environment either as a student or administrator. He recently accepted his first role outside of academia. At work Peter is often complimented on his ability to see the big picture, breaking problems and issues down into more manageable pieces. Peter works for a major education foundation that allows him to tackle the Urban Education issue in the manner he's always dreamed. Peter is very strategic, analytic and detail-oriented. However, Peter doesn't suffer fools. His upbringing has also taught him to see things in very black and white terms. To Peter, either something is or it isn't, there is little in between.

Two months ago, his boss left and he got a new boss. Though his work is top notch, Peter and his new boss don't get along. Under his previous boss, Peter functioned with very little supervision. Peter had complete autonomy, he made the decisions where his program was concerned and he rarely had to run his actions by someone for approval. His boss had complete trust in his actions and his decision-making. This isn't the case with the new guy. As a result, Peter is struggling at work.

Not only is this his new boss' first time leading a team but he also does not have nearly the educational background or credentials that Peter possesses. Add to that the fact that he is constantly micromanaging Peter. In Peter's estimation, his boss does not have the credentials to do this work, much less to supervise someone with Peter's background. Peter doesn't believe his new boss even understands the foundational issues of the work they need to accomplish. Peter believes his boss' tactical manner is not only unfitting of someone in a leadership position but is also unfocused, counterproductive, and ineffective, leading to what Peter believes are some very costly errors to their work. Their inability to work as an effective unit is causing the team to lose progress and setting their work behind. Peter's frustrations are often apparent in every interaction he has with his new boss.

BROOKE
Finance executive who has decided to take a step back in order to break into a new industry.

Brooke left an executive level Finance position with a major museum to accept a mid-level professional position with a major airline. Since she was switching sectors, she knew she needed to accept a lower position to get her foot in the door. Despite this, she was confident that she would soon make a positive name for herself and make her way up the ladder, back to the executive suite.

On her first day, Brooke walked through the glass doors of her new company full of confidence. She was sure the job was going to be a piece of cake. She was confident in her skills and believed she could make an immediate contribution. However, from the onset she seemed to be having trouble assimilating into the corporate environment. Her superiors and colleagues seemed to speak a different language. She was making a lot of small but noticeable mistakes. The work wasn't hard but for some reason she didn't seem to be grasping very basic requests. In her effort to keep up with the fast pace of this new world her attention to detail was suffering. So, she tried harder and, while that worked some of the time, there were still those moments when she didn't feel like she was keeping up with her work. Part of her frustration grew out of the fact that she had been used to doing much higher-level work than she was doing now. She agreed to take a position that paid less, with a job title that wasn't reflective of her vast experience in order to get her foot in the door. But now she was beginning to question how capable she was. If she couldn't complete some of the simple tasks that were being asked of her, how would she ever be given greater responsibility?

What do Nicole, Peter, and Brooke all have in common? They are all workers trying to find success in the new economy.

Nicole had been with the financial institution for 13 years. Having that type of tenure had allowed her to learn the ins and outs of their systems by utilizing them, first as a teller and then as an assistant branch manager, prior to moving into the training department. In her new company, she was expected to learn in eight weeks what had taken her eight years to learn at the financial institution.

In Peter's situation, he was also being asked to understand the world of work in a new way. Peter was being asked to learn the leadership style of a new manager and to take direction from someone who worked in a manner that Peter didn't value. Peter's work style was very deliberate and thorough, typical of an academic. As a new manager, his new boss was used to reacting and responding to anything and everything.

And, Brooke. To find the success she had grown accustomed to, she needed to quickly learn a completely new environment, one based on speed and agility. Every day it seemed as if things were never the same as the day before. She had to learn to constantly adjust and respond to the newness and still produce a quality product at a moment's notice.

These workers are no different than the rest of the American workforce. Nicole, the company "steady Eddie," who decides to leave the comfort and stability of what she's known for more money in an unknown environment, only to find herself a fish out of water. Or Peter, an academic powerhouse, in the job of his dreams, who sees the world in very black and white terms. Now add to the equation a frustrating boss who appears to be making it up as he goes along. Finally, there's Brooke, a talented go-getter who is beginning to drown in her own quicksand of self-doubt.

All three must confront and adjust to a new work environment. A workplace characterized by constant change, increasing complexity, speed and ambiguity. The trouble is none of them have an instruction manual, a roadmap to help them navigate these unknown waters. Still if they don't figure things out soon they each may be looking for new employment or relegated to a position of ineffectualness or obscurity. Though they all work for very different organizations they are each faced with the same challenge, finding the answer to the question," What *does it mean to be successful in today's economy?"*

Now, let's get to the rules.

THE
RULES

RULE #1: MAKE YOUR HUSTLE MATTER

"Your work is going to fill a large part of your life, and the only way to be truly satisfied is to do what you believe is great work. And the only way to do great work is to love what you do. If you haven't found it yet, keep looking. Don't settle. As with all matters of the heart, you'll know when you find it. And, like any great relationship, it just gets better and better as the years roll on. So, keep looking until you find it. Don't settle."
- Steve Jobs

What happens when the thing you've wanted to do your whole life becomes the thing you can't stand to do for one more minute? We've all heard the stories of Harvard-trained attorneys who wake up one day and want to teach in urban schools. Or tech geeks who decide to transition from programming code to pastry making. At some point, many of us come to that career crossroad when we say to ourselves, "If I'm going to spend 10-12 hours a day doing anything I want to do something that feeds my soul, something that makes my heart sing.

So how do you make it happen? How do you find your calling?

You start by thinking strategically. Determining where you want to go in your career is all about creating a vision, defining your mission, and identifying the strategic goals and objectives that will take you there. Approaching your career with this mindset is no different than the way companies create their own strategic planning processes. You are the product and your employer is the customer. It's a simple five step process:

Step 1: Know thyself
Step 2: Identify what's important
Step 3: Define what you must achieve
Step 4: Establish who is accountable
Step 5: Review & refine

Let's take each of these steps individually:

Step 1: Know thyself.

This begins with self-awareness. Self-awareness requires recognition of what you bring to the table. This starts with clearly identifying your strengths or talents as well as the areas where you need to improve, sometimes referred to as opportunities or weaknesses.

For many of us this is harder than it sounds since we are unsure of what our true talents and strengths are. We've spent our lives being programmed to focus on what's wrong with us. We've been told that, to get better, we need to fix our weaknesses. As a result, most people, when asked, can deliver a mini-sermon on our faults. We have a PhD in our shortcomings. Yet, when asked to define what we are really great at, we have trouble. This is a direct result of our early socialization. We've been trained almost since birth to correct our flaws, not to focus on our talents. Anyone who's ever played sports knows this is true. Fumble a pass, miss a free throw in a game, or drop the baton and you'll spend the next few practices making up for that mistake. Think about it. It wasn't the A on the report card that got much of your parent's attention, it was that pesky D.

Don't get me wrong, we need to know what our opportunities are. But, only so we don't allow them to derail us, not so we can devote every waking moment to attending to them. No, what's more important is that we get really good at identifying and spending time developing those things that we are great at. At the same time, with regard to our weaknesses, we need to distinguish between those things that are real derailers and have the potential to limit our career progress and those things that are bothersome but have no bearing on our future potential. From there, our approach should be to achieve the right balance of focusing our development time on continuous improvement around our strengths and neutralizing those annoying career stallers.

Think about it this way: in basketball, a great point guard would not be served by trying to be a great power forward. Instead, if that same point guard spent time focused on developing his natural talents, he has a greater likelihood of turning his previously great performance into one of excellence. So, rather than spending his practice time improving his rebounding ability, a better use of his time would be to spend it developing his ball handling skills, court vision (or play calling) and execution. This doesn't mean he shouldn't work on rebounding. It's just probably not where he should spend most his time. "When we're able to put most of our energy into developing our natural talents, extraordinary room for growth exists. So, a revision to the "You-can-be-anything-you-want-to-be" maxim might be more accurate: You cannot be anything you want to be—but you can be a lot more of who you already are," Tom Rath, *StrengthsFinder 2.0*.

During the strategic planning process, many companies use a SWOT (Strengths, Weaknesses, Opportunities & Threats) analysis to assess their strengths and weaknesses, as well as the opportunities and threats they face in the competitive environment. The SWOT analysis is a proven tool for companies and is also a great tool for your individual development. By taking a very objective approach to answering some key questions, the SWOT can help you zero in in your personal career strategy and figure out how to realize your short- and long-term career goals.

Conducting an effective SWOT is all about asking yourself the right questions:

Strengths *What do you excel at?*	Weaknesses *What hinders you from top performance?*
Opportunities *What external factors create a favorable advantage for you?*	**Threats** *What external factors have the potential to negatively impact your success?*

Strengths:
- What do you do better than anyone else?
- What do *other* people say you do well?

Weaknesses:
- What don't you do well?

- What feedback have others given you about what you need to improve?

Opportunities:
- What could be done today that isn't being done?
- Is there a need in your department that no one is meeting?
- What could you do today that isn't being done?
- How is your field changing? How can you take advantage of those changes?

Threats:
- Who is competing with you for projects or roles? What do they have that you don't?
- Is there a change in demand for what you do?

While the SWOT analysis is a proven tool, there are many ways to get clear on who you are and what you bring to the table. There are books, like *StrengthsFinder 2.0*, that will help identify what those talents are. Another strategy is to review past performance evaluations. This allows you to look for themes in the feedback you've received. What things were called out as strengths? What types of work did you gravitate to and what were the outcomes? Another approach many people employ is to take behavioral or personality tests. These enable you to make predictions about how you will respond across a range of vastly different work-related activities. These predictions can assist in determining how suitable you are for certain roles.

The message here is that there are many places where you can and should gather feedback. Doing this will help you prioritize your development actions by uncovering your strengths, neutralizing your weaknesses, and zeroing in on the work you really want to do.

Step 2: Identify what's important.

Now get clear about why you are working. As Clayton Christensen writes in *How Will You Measure Your Life*, "...if the decisions you make about where you invest your blood, sweat, and tears are not consistent with the person you aspire to be, you'll never become that person." Some people work because of the life that it affords them and others work because they enjoy the satisfaction of being a part of something. Is a high salary important to you? Is it important for your work to involve interacting with people? Would you like your work to contribute to society? Is having a prestigious job most important for you? It's also crucial to note that your motivations will change over the lifecycle of your career. What you are motivated by in your 20s may be very different from what you want in your 30s or 40s. Whatever your motivations are you should be clear about how your job impacts your attainment of those desires.

Once you are clear about your motivations you then need to determine your baseline expectations. Expectations may revolve around your raises, your promotability, your work/life balance, etc. The key is that your motivations and expectations should be aligned with each other. For instance, if you are motivated to become CEO of a Fortune 500 company, your expectations of the hours that you will put in and the sacrifices you will have to make to ascend to that level must be aligned with one another. You'll never be the CEO of a Fortune 500 company coming in at 9 and leaving at 5. It's just not going to happen. So, you need to decide which desire means more: working 9-5 or being a Fortune 500 CEO. All too often people want the corner office but they are unrealistic about the time, effort, and sacrifice it takes to sit in that chair.

Step 3: Define what you must achieve.

Remember when you were 10 and your aspirations to be an astronaut, teacher, nuclear physicist, clown, and compete in the Olympics seemed completely plausible? Then you got a little older and realized how much you loved books so you decided to be an English Lit major. But once you graduated you couldn't find a job. Then one day, while drowning your sorrows in a double chocolate mocha Frappuccino, a guy sits next to you and you can't help but overhear his intriguing phone conversation. he gets off the phone you muster up the nerve to ask him what he does for a living and he says he's in pharmaceutical sales. You ask a few more questions, the two of you exchange information and three months later you have your own sales territory, a wonder drug, and a six-figure income.

Sounds crazy, right? Maybe twenty years ago, but not today. We all know those people who started off thinking they were headed down one path and an inner gnawing, a chance encounter, a speech at a seminar, a magazine article, or some other random occurrence sends them in a completely different direction. Once there, it's as if the moon and the stars aligned and they've found some sort of professional career Nirvana. That's generally what sets the truly successful apart from others. They've found their unique place in the world, the place where their natural skills, talents, and interest converge with the right opportunity and environment. And, if this place doesn't exist, then they will build it.

Often the problem is that we make finding our paths harder than it should be. We think mapping our career trajectory requires some magic potion, a lot of money, or something else we don't have. It doesn't. As Jon Acuff writes in *Quitter*, "Sometimes we think we need a massive eureka moment to come to grips with who we want to be and what we want to do. We wait for the lightning strike that will completely redefine our lives and give us clear direction, but the truth is the greatest impacts tend to come from those smaller moments...a chance encounter at the grocery store, a random comment from a stranger, a line in a book...," he goes on to add, "Do more of the things you love and less of the things you like. Make your hustle matter."

Now that you've done the analysis, here's how to find your hustle:

- Review the SWOT analysis.
- Figure out what gets you excited.
- Draw a hypothesis about the synergies between what you are good at (strengths) and what excites you.
- Collect data. Are there people you can talk to who are doing this kind of work? Books you can read? How can you validate?
- Test your hypothesis. Are there ways that you can see this work in action? Can you shadow someone who is already doing the work?
- Test your hypothesis again. Does this work exist with your current employer? Can you volunteer? Can you work part-time? Can you start your own business doing the work?

The self-discovery process truly can't be overstated. As Angela Duckworth notes in her book, *Grit: Passion, Perseverance, and the Science of Success,* without figuring out what kindles our fire, what causes us to come alive, we'll flounder about, hoping that, through some cosmic aligning of the stars, it will all come together. "...interests are not discovered through introspection. Instead, interests are triggered by interactions with the outside world. The process of interest discovery can be messy, serendipitous, and inefficient. This is because you can't really predict with certainty what will capture your attention and what won't...Without experimenting, you can't figure out which interests will stick, and which won't."

Figuring out your path is critical, on both a personal and professional level. According to Simon Sinek in *Start with Why: How Great Leaders Inspire Everyone to Take Action.*

"Studies show that over 80 percent of Americans do not have their dream job. If more knew how to build organizations that inspire, we could live in a world in which that statistic was the reverse — a world in which over 80 percent of people loved their jobs. People who love going to work are more productive and more creative. They go home happier and have happier families. They treat their colleagues and clients and customers better. Inspired employees make for stronger companies and stronger economies."

Step 4: Gain clarity.

Sometimes all you can see is the destination. That makes the hustle hard. Is it truly realistic to go from the position you're in today to the CEO chair? Probably not.

Do research on your company and chosen industry to see the career path and corresponding steps that lead to the position you aspire to hold. Then do your research:

- How many positions are between your current position and the one you want to occupy?
- What will it take for you to get to each of those positions?
- What is your focus at each position? Do you need leadership experience, international exposure, skill development, or something else?
- How will you get to each of these roles? Can you do this in your current functional area or will you need to move (for instance, leaving the Finance team to work in Strategic Planning)?? Will you need a transfer (for instance, staying in Human Resources, but leaving the Compensation team and transferring to the Benefits team)? Maybe a relocation is necessary? Perhaps it's a move to a completely new company that you need.

The only way to clearly map out your path is to be clear on what your aspiration is. So, go ahead, set your intention and get busy mapping out your strategy.

Step 5: Determine who is accountable.

This is the easy part. In a word, this is you. Others can help, but the only person who is accountable is you. "Human beings, individually or collectively cannot transform or uplift themselves without taking full responsibility for doing so. This is a law of nature. Once full responsibility is accepted others can assist if it is understood that they cannot be responsible. No group in history has been lifted into excellence or competitiveness by another group."- Shelby Steele

Step 6: Review & refine.

Once you've gotten clear about what your path is, write it down. As the writers of *Change Anything* revealed, "Repeated studies show that simply writing down a plan increases your chance of success by more than 30 percent." Once you've written it down, the only thing left is to do it.

If you go through the exercise and still feel conflicted, share your thoughts with a friend or trusted colleague to get their input. Most importantly, remember that careers today are not linear, they wind and they curve. Give yourself time, it'll come together.

NOW, GET TO WORK!

Do this...
- If you haven't done it yet, conduct a SWOT analysis.
- Figure out your path.
- Identify 2-3 areas where you want to develop. Create a development plan to address those areas.

Answer these questions...
- What type of lifestyle do you want to have? What sacrifices will that require of you? Are you willing to make those sacrifices? What will the reward be?
- Take a stab at writing down your ideal work situation. What type of work are you doing? Are you working independently or as a member of a team? Are you in an office environment? Who do you report to? Who reports to you? Be as detailed as you can.
- Think back on past conversations and the feedback you've been given. What are your strengths? How have you leveraged these strengths in the past? What actions do you need to employ to take your strengths from good to great?
- What areas do you need to improve in that could potentially derail you? What actions do you need to take to neutralize these areas so they don't become derailers?

Notes:

Mantra to Master

"When a child is learning how to walk and falls down 50 times, they never think to themselves, 'Maybe this isn't for me.' "

Lewis Howes

RULE #2:
MIND YOUR
BUSINESS

"The assumption on which the organization has been built and is being run no longer fits reality."
– Peter Drucker

Is it impossible for you to start the day without your Grande Skinny Mocha Latte from Starbucks? Or are you often running late in the morning because you can't decide which pair of black shoes to wear? If either of these scenarios sound familiar then you understand a little about the new market forces that companies must confront.

What this should get you thinking about is the competitive standards we discussed earlier. It is those standards that drive why you need a Starbucks when everyone including the local gas station is selling coffee. It should also show you that it is not enough to only understand what happens in the walls of your cubicle. To be successful, you must understand what differentiates your company and what the relevant business situation your company and your industry is facing. This is imperative because you want everything you do to be align with or drive the company's strategic intentions.

Awareness of the business situation is acquired by becoming astutely aware of the strategic direction of your company. Strategy is what sets your organization apart from its competitors. Strategy is about understanding the culture, processes, and systems of the organization in which you work. It involves a combination of planning, interaction, evaluation, and adjustment and is continually reshaped as market conditions change. This reshaping process requires leaders to anticipate and respond to customer needs and a constantly-evolving economic environment.

In *Playing To Win: How strategy really works*, A.G. Lafley describes strategy this way: "A strategy is a coordinated and integrated set of five choices: a winning aspiration, where to play, how to win, core capabilities, and management systems." He goes on to add, "Strategy needn't be mysterious. Conceptually, it is simple and straightforward. It requires clear and hard thinking, real creativity, courage, and personal leadership."

You need to be knowledgeable of how your company makes and responds to these five choices. Having a command of your company's strategy will allow you to fully comprehend how the leadership team identifies the right initiatives to respond to a changing and complex business environment. This will enable you to identify how your work aligns to the success of your company and ensure that you are focused on the right work every day.

When assessing the business situation, you should be able to answer the following questions:
- What are our company's values?
- What is our vision? Mission?

- What do we do?
- How do we make money?
- What are our core competencies?
- What is our market?
- Who are our customers?
- Why do they buy our products/services?
- Who are our competitors?
- What are the two or three organizational imperatives that, if done well, will have a significant positive impact on the business and if left undone will have a significant detrimental impact on the business?

Ok, I can hear you groaning. Don't throw your hands up just yet. You don't need an MBA to understand strategy. There are several proven methods for getting the knowledge you need.

1. **Ask.** Schedule time with someone in Finance and ask them to walk you through the company's financial reports. Meet with someone in Marketing and have them walk you through the marketing plan. Identify others in the organization who own a key piece of the strategy puzzle and spend time with them to better understand what they do.

2. **Read.** Leaders are readers. Period. Set up a Google alert to funnel articles directly to your inbox regarding your company, its competitors, and the industry. Subscribe to magazines and trade journals within your industry as well as your profession. Find out what books leaders in your company are reading and read those, too.

3. **Join.** Industry groups and professional organizations are great places to stay abreast of the latest news or economic changes that might impact your company. Sign up for a LinkedIn group related to your industry or profession.

4. **Enroll.** Ultimately you may decide that additional schooling would be beneficial. Or maybe you just need a certification or additional training.

Grasping the relevant business situation is really about demonstrating your business acumen. Leaders in your company want to see that you have a firm command of budgets, profit and loss, and return on investment. They want to see that you have a strategic mindset and that you understand how the work you are doing aligns with the bigger picture. They want to be certain you know when to make tough decisions and that you will be frugal with scarce resources, ensuring that you get the biggest impact from the resources entrusted to you.

NOW, GET TO WORK!

Do this...
- Read: *A Whole New Mind*, Daniel Pink

Answer these questions...
- What is the current business situation in your company or industry?
- What is the one thing you need to do today to start thinking more strategically?
- How are the competitive requirements impacting your company/industry? How is your company responding? Discuss in detail.

Notes:

Life in the Real World

Company Strategy: Home Depot

In December of 2000, Home Depot installed a new CEO, to meet his strategic goals; the new CEO had to build an organization that understood the opportunity in, and the importance of, taking advantage of its growing scale. Some functions, such as purchasing, needed to be centralized to leverage the buying power that a giant company could wield. And a new emphasis needed to be placed on employee training, not only to bolster the managerial ranks but also to transform orange-aproned sales associates from cheerful greeters into knowledgeable advisors who could help customers solve their home improvement problems. This new strategy would require a careful renovation of Home Depot's strong culture. Employees would need to start relying on data, not on intuition to assess business and marketplace conditions. People needed to coordinate their efforts, which didn't traditionally happen in their entrepreneurial culture. People needed to be accountable to companywide financial and other targets, not hostile towards them. People needed to deliver not just sales growth, but also other components of business performance that drive profitability.

Excerpted from, *Home Depot's Blueprint for Culture Change*, Harvard Business Review. April 2006.

What does the new direction for Home Depot mean for its current employees?

What type of skills will be critical to the success of this new strategy?

What is the one thing you need to do today to begin thinking more strategically?

Notes

Mantra to Master

"Trust that little voice in your head that says, 'wouldn't it be great if…' and then do it."

Marie Forleo, life coach & motivational speaker

RULE #3: PIE RULES EVERYTHING AROUND ME

"Without ambition one starts nothing. Without work one finishes nothing. The prize will not be sent to you. You have to win it."
— **Ralph Waldo Emerson**

Remember the story I shared earlier, where I was drowning on the new job and couldn't figure out why? I wish I could say that all it took were those inspirational words from my co-worker and, poof, things were different. But, I can't. Those words served as a catalyst, but I had serious work to do.

I needed a new strategy, a formula for success. As I shared earlier, I started looking around my environment determining who the successful people were. The people who I could learn from and emulate. What I saw in them lined up with research from CEB. They have done significant research on what differentiates Hi-Pos from solid performers. According to their research, high-potential employees have three characteristics in common: aspiration, ability and engagement.

1. Aspiration is the desire to take on responsibilities, challenges and rewards typically demonstrated by those in more senior roles. The key question to answer is: Do you have the desire to grow and do more in your organization?
2. Ability is the single greatest predictor of success. It is a combination of innate characteristics and learned skills. Ability is linked to the knowledge and skills required to function within your job and your organization. The key question to answer is: Can you perform in more senior roles in the organization?)
3. Engagement is the extent to which you value, enjoy, and believe in your organization. The extent to which you believe that staying with your organization is in their self-interest. The key question to answer is: Are you attached to the organization and willing to go "above and beyond" the call of duty?

The people I identified had all 3 of these and two more characteristics in common. The additional characteristics were: Behaviors and Execution.

4. Behaviors are closely linked to ability. They are how you accomplish your job. The key question to answer is how do you do the job? Do you do it in a way that inspires others or do you leave a trail of dead bodies as you get things done?
5. Execution is your ability to get results by bringing these forces together in a way that consistently adds value and supports the organization's attainment of it's strategy. The key question to answer is: Are you accountable and can you deliver meaningful results for the organization?

My observations led me to a new formula for performance:

(Ability + Behaviors + Aspiration + Engagement) X Execution = Breakthrough Performance

Now that I had a vision for success I rolled up my sleeves and went to work. First, I made sure my work was impeccable, but I also understood that it didn't always have to be finished. By leaving my work slightly unfinished I created opportunities, where appropriate, to seek feedback and input from my boss and key colleagues. This small but meaningful act demonstrated my ability to partner with others and my openness to feedback. (More on this later.)

My strategy also included:

- Getting out from behind my desk and building relationships.
- Learning the culture of the organization.
- Volunteering for projects and assignments.
- Taking advantage of EVERY learning opportunity.

I'll share more on each on these tactics later. But in a nutshell, I employed what my friend, Andre, SVP, Human Resources at a leading specialty retailer refers to as the PIE principle: Performance, Image, and Exposure.

The Performance slice of the "PIE" is your entry ticket. This is how you build your reputation, how you start your legacy. Nothing else happens before you solidify yourself as someone who can perform, someone who can be counted on to execute. High performance is the common denominator in the promotion process. A prevailing belief that you have the ability to perform, that people can count on you, confirms your ability to take on more responsibility.

The authors of *Change Anything: The New Science of Personal Success*, describe it this way: "Know your stuff — top performers put regular effort into ensuring that they are good at the technical aspects of their jobs. They work hard at honing their craft. Focus on the right stuff — top

71

performers contribute to tasks that are essential to the organization's success. Build a reputation for being helpful — top people are widely known and respected by others not because of their frequent contact, charm or likability, but because they help others solve their problems."

What it looks like:

- Don't wait for your manager to tell you what you need to know to do your job.
- Manage your own skill development and application. Proactively seek skill development opportunities.
- Assess and define problems you are facing.
- Establish appropriate goals that, if achieved, will solve the problem.
- Monitor the ways in which aspects of your environment are hindering the attainment of your goals.
- Develop a plan for achieving the goals.
- Determine whether the plan is working and revise where necessary.
- Learn new ways of dealing with challenging or new situations.
- Find appropriate ways to manage resources (time, talent, attitudes, etc.).

While you are working to develop a consistent record of exceptional performance, you also need to focus on your image. Image is the message you send before you speak, whether intentional or not. It includes your attire, confidence, and demeanor. When your image is right it telegraphs the message, "I'm ready." While your image begins to develop early in your career, there are strategies you can employ to reform your image. However, the reformation process can be hard. Depending on how deeply entrenched people are in their perception of "who you are," reformation may not be a hill worth climbing. For this reason, you need to do an assessment to truly understand how people see you. Then determine if there are aspects of their perception that need to change in order to help you achieve your aspirations and goals.

Image also requires dressing the part. Yes, the way you look matters.

Simply put, people aren't going to invest in or follow someone who doesn't look the part. Period. This doesn't mean you need to break the bank to keep up with people at a higher pay grade. It doesn't even mean you must change who you are. What it does mean is that you need to survey your environment and see how people one or two levels above you dress and emulate them. What you wore when you were an entry-level assistant won't be appropriate on your way to becoming CEO.

Finally, there's exposure. Exposure is about high career impact. It's how others know of your performance. As Jeffrey Pfeffer notes in *Power: Why Some People Have It and Others Don't*, "Your job is to ensure that those influential others have a strong desire to make you successful. Ensure that those in power notice the good work that you do, remember you, and think well of you because you make them feel good about themselves. It is performance, coupled with political skill, that will help you rise through the ranks."

Exposure gives you the right visibility to those who can influence your career. It is enhanced by your network of mentors, bosses, and sponsors. It is key because, regardless of how talented, accomplished or ready to lead you think you are, having someone of influence and power in your corner is essential. Exposure expands the right people's view of what you are capable of, ensures you have connections and visibility to senior leaders, guarantees that you are getting actionable, specific feedback (the unvarnished facts, both good and bad), and, most importantly, it makes certain that when important conversations about your company's future are being had your name is part of those discussions, in a good way.

I know, I know. You don't want to get ahead based on who you know. You want your work to speak for itself. It's unfair to be rewarded for anything other than merit alone. It just doesn't feel right.

I get it. Really, I do. I was part of that cult for a long time myself. Until I realized, in this day and age, it's an outdated concept. So, let's make a pact. Let's save the "pull yourself up by the bootstraps" tales for Hollywood movies and political speeches. Unless you are content to continue watching others get the coveted promotion, salary increase, or that career building stretch assignment, it's time to realize that hard work alone won't get you the recognition or move you up the career ladder the way you hope.

As Sylvia Ann Hewlett notes in *Executive Presence: The Missing Link Between Merit and Success*, "It is executive presence — and no man or woman attains a top job, lands an extraordinary deal, or develops a significant following without this heady combination of confidence, poise, and authenticity that convinces the rest of us we're in the presence of someone who's the real deal. It's an amalgam of qualities that telegraphs that you are in charge or deserve to be."

The talent development process is the road to getting that exposure and ultimately being viewed as a high-potential employee within your company. Comprehending how your company approaches the process of managing and developing talent (i.e., distorting efforts and resources to the highest potential employees) will give you a leg up on the competition.

Your company will have a corporate view on talent that will include processes such as the performance management process, comprised of midyear reviews, annual reviews, merit increases, talent reviews, and succession planning. The talent development process begins at the recruitment phase and spans the tenure of an employee. It includes all the strategies a company employs to attract, develop, and retain the talent needed to execute its strategy.

As an employee, you need to understand the larger company view on how talent is or isn't developed, who gets developed, and the talent management philosophy. From there you can position yourself in a way that aligns your personal growth strategy to those ideas. For our purposes the talent development process, from the employee's perspective, is defined as taking personal responsibility for understanding the culture, business operations, and initiatives of the company in which you work. Next, it requires aligning these competencies to your unique skill set, knowledge base, and expertise to find that sweet spot where your aspirations, ability, and engagement intersect to create value for your company.

To understand the tenets of adding and creating value think about the relationship between a company and its shareholders. Shareholders buy shares in a business on the stock market, putting capital into that business. What shareholders want is a return (profit) on their investment, usually in the form of dividends or by selling off shares should share value rise.

In the individual value equation, you are the share and your company is looking for a return on its investment (ROI) in you. The more you add meaningful value, the greater ROI.

There are three primary ways to add value:
- **Financial:** Increasing revenue or decreasing costs.
- **Brand:** Enhancing the organization's reputation.
- **Operations:** Improving processes.

Once you identify how what you do affects one or more of these three areas, you must be able to articulate your value. Here's how to get started:

- **Figure out how your company makes money.** Now align your work to that process. Aligning your day to day efforts to the bottom line of your organization positions you as a key contributor.
- **Don't be quick to fix.** If I had a dollar for every time someone told me they were hired to overhaul something, I'd be a billionaire. Everything in your organization isn't broken so stop applying a hammer to everything you touch.
- **Over deliver.** This may mean coming in ahead of the original time promised or doing a little more than you originally agreed to. Remember, if you do decide to do more be sure you get it done at the originally agreed upon deadline.
- **Be known for something that matters.** Having an expertise or skill set that sets you apart and is something that is in demand in your organization will prove beneficial for you and your company.
- **Manage your time.** Time is a valuable commodity in any organization, make sure you are using yours wisely.
- **Raise your hand but make sure you know the answers to the test.** Taking on additional responsibilities demonstrates you're a team player. It also lets you learn and develop new skills. Be sure, when you volunteer for an assignment or when your manager or executives have a question about something you are responsible for you have the answers they need or you know where to get them.

Everyone in an organization can't and won't be a Hi-Po. Some studies suggest that only 3-5% of employees will be viewed in this way. Hi-Pos get more training, have more visibility and time with senior leaders, and are promoted at rates higher than the average employee.

Remember, the key to the PIE principles is that order matters. Lots of people attempt to go straight for exposure, but if you lack substance (i.e., performance) you will eventually reach a ceiling. You must also understand that each principle is interrelated. The performance you have leads to you having impact, which, in turn, gets you the exposure you seek

NOW, GET TO WORK!

Do this...

- Figure out what piece of the PIE you need to develop.
- Determine what area you are better at than anyone else. (Make sure the area has meaning to your organization.) Develop a plan to further develop your expertise in that area.
- Take the Hi-Po assessment on the next page.
- Learn about your organization's talent review/succession planning process. Ask your manager how the organization views you as part of this key process.

Notes:

Life in the
Real World

Hi-Po Assessment
Rate yourself against the following Hi-Po indicators. Determine if you Always (A), Often (O), Sometimes (S), Rarely (R) or Never (N) do these things. Once you take the assessment determine what areas you need to spend time developing in.

	Rating
Ability: Can you perform in more senior roles in the organization?	
Aspiration: Do your career goals and professional expectations align with the responsibilities and demands of more senior, more critical roles?	
Engagement: Are you meaningfully connected to and engaged in the organization?	
Behaviors: Do you lead in a way that inspires others? Does your way of working align with your organizations values?	
Execution: Are you accountable and can you deliver meaningful results for the organization?	
Do you have positive visibility in your company (the right people know your work and think highly of the contributions you have made.)?	
Is your performance rating always meets or exceeds expectations?	
Is your opinion often sought out for solutions to more complex problems and situations?	

The point here is not that you do these things some of the time, but that you do them consistently and in ways that the person in the cubicle next to you doesn't. Everyone in an organization can't and won't be a Hi-Po. Some studies suggest that only 3-5% of employees will be viewed in this way. Hi-Pos get more training, have more visibility and time with senior leaders, and are promoted at rates higher than the average employee.

Notes:

Mantra to Master

"50 told me, go 'head, switch the style up. And if they hate then let 'em hate and watch the money pile up."

Kanye West

RULE #4: DEVELOP A PERFORMANCE POV

"Look, if you had one shot, or one opportunity, to seize everything you ever wanted in one moment, would you capture it or just let it slip?"
– Eminem

It's clear that there are multiple factors, including increased focus on growth, an aging workforce, and increased business complexity that create an imperative for organizations to focus on talent. However, while companies are placing a laser-like focus on talent, too many workers still do not know what it takes to set themselves apart from the pack. Malcolm Gladwell zeroes in on the heart of the matter in *Outliers*, "Once a musician has enough ability to get into a top music school, the thing that distinguishes one performer from another is how hard he or she works. That's it. What's more, the people at the very top don't work just harder or even much harder than everyone else. They work much, much harder." Not only this, there are still too many workers toiling away in positions, waiting for someone to tap them on the head and acknowledge their talent.

Instead of waiting for that moment, today's worker must figure out how to first get hired by a company, then learn the culture and what it takes to be successful, differentiate themselves, and finally move up.

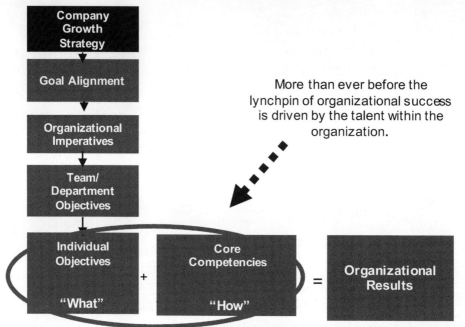

To do this, workers must develop a Performance Point of View (POV) by learning company strategy and the competencies and skills necessary for success. It means being able to envision and employ the systems and processes that create organizational advantage. As the structure of the U.S. economy has shifted, new skill requirements have emerged.

Today's workplaces typically require broader, and often less measurable, general skills like learning, reasoning, communicating, problem-solving, innovation, creative thinking, and other behavioral skills. These skills are not a substitute, but rather a complement to the specific academic and vocational skills that employers demand. As Peter Drucker notes, "People in general, and knowledge workers in particular, grow according to the demands they make on themselves." They grow according to what they consider to be achievement and attainment. If they demand little of themselves, they will remain stunted. If they demand a good deal of themselves, they will grow to giant stature—without any more effort than is expended by the non-achievers."

The knowledge economy relies on these new flexible technologies and high performance work systems that in turn rely on more skilled and autonomous workers. In a time of flexible production systems and rapid economic change workers not only need to be better prepared, they also need sufficiently robust skills to adapt to changing requirements on the job. In the knowledge and creative economies, access to good jobs and higher earnings are acquired by combining the evolving competencies, general education beyond high school (often a college degree, but not always), occupational preparation, and the resultant access to learning and technology on the job.

Because our workplaces are evolving, employees need a clear understanding of the transferable skills and competencies needed to maximize their performance. Competencies act as a guide to identify strengths and opportunities in your capabilities. Knowing the skills required in your field now and in the future, is another component of this principle. Work is ever evolving and the skills required today may or may not be the skills required tomorrow.

Again, Pink from *A Whole New Mind: Why Right-Brainers Will Rule the Future* emphasizes "The future belongs to a very different kind of person with a very different kind of mind—creators and empathizers, pattern recognizers, and meaning makers."

A competency focuses on what is required of an employee in the workplace rather than on the learning process. It embodies the ability to transfer and apply skills and knowledge to new situations and environments. Skills are the abilities acquired by workers through education, training, and experience that enable them to be more productive. Competencies are observable behaviors that demonstrate excellent performance. Competencies are the manifestations of skills that produce successes.

At this point you're probably wondering what these competencies are? Erik Hoffman defines them this way in *New Brain, New World: How the Evolution of a New Human Brain Can Transform Consciousness and Create a New World*, "Today, the defining skills of the previous era — the "left brain" capabilities that powered the Information Age — are necessary but no longer sufficient. And the capabilities we once disdained or thought frivolous — the "right-brain" qualities of inventiveness, empathy, joyfulness, and meaning — increasingly will determine who flourishes and who flounders,"

Educator Tony Wagner is also a proponent of this same thinking and has coined the Seven Survival Skills. They are:

- Critical thinking and problem solving
- Collaboration
- Agility
- Initiative and entrepreneurship
- Effective communication
- Ability to access information
- Curiosity and imagination

Need more evidence that leading companies are moving beyond the litmus tests of the past to determine fit and zeroing in on these skills instead? Let's look at Google. In a 2013 interview with the New York Times, Laszlo Bock, Senior Vice President of People Operations at Google, shared that the company had spent a great deal of time studying who succeeded and who didn't. What it learned fundamentally shaped how it sought out talent. Gone was the focus on GPAs and brand name schools. What replaced this focus on credentials was a focus on the skills, like the ones espoused by Pink and Wagner. In 2014, 14% of Google's workforce did not have college degrees.

"For every job, though, the No. 1 thing we look for is general cognitive ability, and it's not IQ. It's learning ability. It's the ability to process on the fly. It's the ability to pull together disparate bits of information," stated Bock.

Bock goes on to say, "The second is leadership — in particular emergent leadership as opposed to traditional leadership. Traditional leadership is, were you president of the chess club? Were you vice president of sales? How quickly did you get there? We don't care. What we care about is, when faced with a problem and you're a member of a team, do you, at the appropriate time, step in and lead. And just as critically, do you step back and stop leading, do you let someone else? Because what's critical to be an effective leader in this environment is you have to be willing to relinquish power."

Finally, he adds, "It's feeling the sense of responsibility, the sense of ownership, to step in and to try to solve any problem — and the humility to step back and embrace the better ideas of others. Your end goal is what can we do together to problem-solve. I've contributed my piece, and then I step back."

Developing a performance point of view requires willingness to invest the time and effort to build expertise in your craft. Today, success means being both a generalist and a specialist. It means having a broad range of knowledge about many areas in business and how they interrelate as well as a depth of knowledge in your specific job function.

NOW, GET TO WORK!

Do this...

- Assess your performance. Are you consistently operating at the top of your game? If not, what do you need to do to elevate your performance?
- Determine what the key competencies in your organization and job function are. Assess your performance against them. What areas are strengths? What areas require development?
- Seek additional feedback from your manager and trusted peers?
- Assess your current responsibilities and assign deadlines to any current goals that don't have them.
- Write down your most important priorities and post your list in plain view.
- Ask about your organization's expected results. How does your role contribute to expected outcomes?
- **Read:** Maximum Achievement: Strategies and Skills That Will Unlock Your Hidden Powers To Succeed by Brian Tracy
- **Read:** The Breakthrough Imperative: How the Best Managers Get «Outstanding Results by Mark Gottfredson and Steve Schaubert

Notes:

Life in the Real World

Process to Understand: Performance Management

One of the most anxiety producing moments in the life of most employee is the annual performance review. Even the highest performing of employees can feel a sense of dread when the time turns once again to this discussion. So, what's the deal? Why do people dread what should be an empowering and enlightening discussion?

There are several factors that cause many to roll their eyes when it comes to the annual review:

1. The conversation. For many this is the first time they've received any feedback either good or bad. So, getting the feedback at the end of the year when there's really no opportunity to affect any change can be demoralizing.
2. The rating. People get so caught up in the number that they can't focus on the conversation.
3. The reflection. The pace of work these days makes it challenging to remember what you did or didn't do a year later.
4. Human nature. Eighty percent of what we hear during the review might be stellar, but we'll spend 100% of time on the twenty percent of negative feedback,

Many companies are finally acknowledging the challenges with how we manage performance and are either doing away with or overhauling their process. Still the annual review continues to be a mainstay at many companies. With this in mind, it's important to get over the dread associated with the practice and make it a more empowering and productive process.

The idea behind the performance review is a worthy one. The goal is to provide feedback, clearly communicate expectations and open a dialogue between managers and employees. Performance reviews give employees and employers a chance to evaluate regularly whether they are happy with each other. The review meeting is a time to evaluate what you did and how you did it over the last year. It's a time set aside for you and your boss to confirm you're both on the same page and to begin laying the foundation for the year to come. The conversation should focus on not only your results but also your performance against the company's values and competencies. So, how do you get comfortable and make the most out of the discussion?

Pre-Review Discussion

Start by understanding how your company handles the process. Sometimes the not knowing is what causes the anxiety. The more you understand the ins and outs of the process, the more likely you are to feel in control of the outcome.

This begins with being clear on your role in the organization. Refer to your job description regularly, and if you have questions, ask them.

Next, you'll need to establish your goals. You should do this as early as possible. Your goals should align with the goals and priorities of your direct supervisor. They should also align with the strategic priorities of your company. Take an initial stab at drafting these and then meet with your manager to confirm them.

Once you and your manager have agreed on the goals, you should create regularly check in points where you can confirm with your manager that you are meeting or exceeding expectations and where you might need to make adjustments. You'll also want to confirm that the goals as established still make sense. Is the business making a turn? Are there new strategic priorities? Making sure that what you're working on still matters is essential to mastering the performance review process.

You'll also want a method to document your accomplishments. As previously mentioned, it's easy to forget the great stuff you've done if you wait until the end of the year. To keep from falling into this trap, keep a log of key milestones. Use your Outlook calendar to also help you keep track of the work that you've been involved in. Focus on strategic outcomes not activities. You'll also want to keep emails or notes you've received when someone offered you positive feedback on your accomplishments and contributions.

Review Time

Now that you've done all the right stuff throughout the year and leading up to the review. It's now time to get ready for the actual conversation.

The formal review process generally starts with you completing a self-evaluation. The self-evaluation is your opportunity to tell your story. Even though you're driving the narrative, the self-evaluation can prove challenging. You want to represent yourself well without bragging or coming across as lacking objectivity. They key is to be honest with yourself about how you have performed in your role. Review the notes you've been keeping throughout the year. Review your calendar again making sure you haven't missed any of your key accomplishments, times when you have exceeded expectations, where you have gone above and beyond your job description. You'll also want to be objective by looking at areas where you have stumbled and missed the mark. Everyone has moments they wish they could do over again. Being honest about those is a quality most managers are looking to see you demonstrate.

Once you've completed your portion of the self-evaluation, your manager will do his part and then he will schedule time for the two of you to sit down and have the official conversation.

For starters, be sure that you are at your best the day of your conversation. Go into the conversation with a positive, optimistic mindset. If possible leave yourself 30 minutes of unscheduled time before the review discussion. This will allow you to clear your mind of anything that may serve as a distraction.

Once the conversation starts you'll want to do more listening than talking. While this is a conversation and there will be opportunities for you to offer input, you should wait and take the lead from your boss. He'll set the tone and create the environment for two-way dialogue. You'll also want to be sure not to be defensive. Again, we're all human and sometimes even constructive criticism is hard to hear. Focusing on defending your position or refuting your boss' point of view won't create the type of learning and growth opportunities that will ultimately create the most benefit for you. Also avoid shifting blame. Blaming someone else is never the right strategy. Talk in a calm, factual manner, rather than a defensive or emotional way.

The final phase of the review process is mapping the path ahead. Not only are you going to want to align on the coming year, but this is an opportune time to discuss the long-term options available to you.

- **Promotions & Raises:** Many companies separate the promotion and compensation process from the review discussion. Despite this, it is still appropriate to talk with your boss about how you'll get to the next level. This begins by you sharing your commitment to growing and developing with the organization. Then you'll want to ask for your manager's feedback on the specific timing for getting to that next step.

- **Short-Term Goals:** Coming out of the review you want to understand clearly how you should be spending your time over the next 30, 60, 90 days. What your focus and priorities are for the next year. Your goal is to meet or exceed expectations so getting off to a great start is critical.
- **Areas for Development:** No matter how stellar your review, there are surely opportunities for you to get better. Now is the time to ask your manager what those areas are. Link these to your short and long-term career aspirations.

Notes:

Mantra to Master

"You wanna fly, you got to give up the shit that weighs you down."

Toni Morrison,
Song of Solomon

BROOKE'S DILEMMA

Remember Brooke from earlier? Brooke left a position with a nonprofit organization to accept a position with a major retail corporation. When Brooke first started, she was confident that the job was going to be a piece of cake. She was confident in her skills and believed that she could make an immediate contribution. However, from the beginning she seemed to have trouble assimilating into the corporate environment. She was making a lot of minor mistakes. The work wasn't hard, but for some reason she didn't seem to be grasping some very basic things. In her effort to keep up with the fast pace of the world she was in her attention to detail was suffering. So, she tried harder. While this worked some of the time, there were still those moments when she didn't feel like she was staying in front of her work.

If she couldn't complete the simple tasks that were being asked of her, how was she ever going to be given the greater responsibility she desired?

Based on what you've read so far, what advice would you give Brooke?

RULE #5: ADAPT TO AMBIGUITY

"If things start happening, don't worry, don't stew, just go right along and you'll start happening too."
- Dr. Seuss

We've all heard the phrase "change is the only constant." As business becomes more and more complex the level of change will only increase. Despite the vast amount of change we all face we all know change isn't easy. It often brings with it varying degrees of ambiguity. Ambiguity creates complexity which can often make decision-making difficult. Additionally, ambiguity often leads to anxiety and confusion.

As you move up in an organization your ability to work in ambiguous situations should improve. Many of us spend considerable time wishing and hoping our organizations would change; however, when change finally comes it's often not what we were hoping for, leaving us wholly unprepared or unready to respond. However, it's not enough to just deal with ambiguity and change. The real skill is being able to make consistently good decisions with often limited information. "Success emerges from the quality of the decisions we make and the quantity of luck we receive. We can't control luck. But we can control the way we make choices," explains Chip & Dan Heath in *Decisive: How to Make Better Choices in Life and Work*.

So how do you become effective managing through the constant change swirling around you?

For starters, it helps to be aware of how the change process works and, more importantly, how you cope with change. One of the most resonant depictions of how we all manage through change is the Kubler Ross Change Curve:

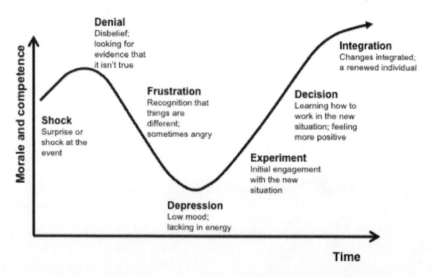

"Life is no straight and easy corridor along which we travel free and unhampered, but a maze of passages, through which we must seek our way, lost and confused, now and again checked in a blind alley. But always, if we have faith, a door will open for us, not perhaps one that we ourselves would ever have thought of, but one that will ultimately prove good for us," Spencer Johnson, *Who Moved My Cheese?*

Understanding the phases of change and how you deal with it is key to becoming adept at effectively managing through anything that comes your way. You must consider two basic principles regarding how we deal with change: 1. our response is personal and 2. it is predictable. It is personal in that we all manage change in our own unique ways. My response to change won't be the same as yours. Our response to change is largely driven by our own filters, attitudes, talents, etc. It is predictable in that we generally have similar emotions and reactions to change.

To get clear on your personal readiness for change ask yourself the following questions:

- Do I understand the value this change will make to business results?
- Do I understand the real impact this change will have on me, my team, and the work we do?
- Do I have the developmental support I need to implement the change and promote any new thinking and behavior that will be required?
- Do I know how and where to get the feedback I need so I know if I am making progress daily and weekly toward key pre-determined milestones?
- Do I have a way to ask for the support I need when I encounter problems?

Now that you understand how you respond to change, next you must believe in your ability to control and direct the aspects of the situation under your oversight. While there will be some situations you won't be able to control, the one thing you'll always be able to control is your response. Great managers of change have developed a constructive 'internal monologue.' This internal monologue is constantly reinforcing your power and asserting your ability to positively manage through whatever comes your way. By cultivating this positive internal monologue, your mindset shifts to a realization that solutions to problems always exist and your goal is to find them and believe that they can be successfully implemented.

To activate this transformation, you should stop seeing ambiguity and change as negative, but instead see them as an opening or white space, a place for you to create. With every change that comes, it brings with it the chance for you to get better, to be innovative, to experiment, and try new approaches to how you do your work. This type of positive mentality creates an environment that will allow you to thrive in the midst of ambiguous situations.

Think of the decisions that are made as the pass is thrown from the quarterback to the receiver. In a football game, the receiver has a split second to catch the ball. There is no time for extensive data analysis and number crunching. There is no one to answer that one last question. Nope, in that moment it's game time. You trust your training, you trust the play calling and when its time you either catch the ball or you don't.

Even the most Zen of us like to feel in control of our environment and the work we do. However, we've all had that desire for control disrupted when ambiguity enters the scene. The reality is that the business world is getting more complex, not less, and therefore we must release our desire to control everything.

In an ambiguous world, it's impossible to wait for the complete picture before we act. If your strategy is to wait for perfection, to need all the hard data before you can act, get over it. Get as much data as is available to you, make the best decision you can and move forward.

As a result, you'll have to be okay with the fact that some of your decisions will be wrong. Don't let that put you off. Being a good business person is about making more right decisions than you do wrong. Get comfortable with making mistakes by looking at them as learning opportunities. This may seem easier said than done, but the more you practice this the better and more comfortable you'll be.

To cultivate this skill, you need to be adept at:

- Assessing and moving through the information you have. Develop a system for making small but quick decisions, getting feedback, course correcting where necessary, and then repeating the process.
- Be disciplined and organized. There will always be more data. If you don't have tight priorities and guardrails you'll be easily led astray.
- Stay focused on the problem at hand. Having a solid grasp of the problem you are trying to solve is key. This will allow you to avoid creep. A common rule of thumb is to keep asking yourself why and make sure you consistently have a plausible answer.

That's how decision-making occurs in an increasingly complex business environment. So, trust your training. Trust your knowledge. Then go execute.

NOW, GET TO WORK!

Do this...

- Assess your comfort working in ambiguous spaces. Practice getting comfortable with ambiguity by making small decisions with little information.
- Consider a decision you need to make. Don't attach to strongly to your first idea. Allow additional ideas to come. Stay flexible and suspend immediate judgment.
- **Read**: *Just Start: Take Action, Embrace Uncertainty, Create the Future* by Leonard A. Schlesinger, Charles F. Kiefer, Paul B. Brown
- **Read:** *Leading Change* by John P. Kotter
- **Read:** *Managing Transitions* by William Bridges

Notes:

Life in the
Real World

Relevant Business Situation & Key Competencies: Toyota

For 20 years Toyota had been dabbling with the idea of placing a traditional gasoline motor alongside an electric one powered by batteries that are recharged whenever the car coasts or brakes. However, there was a split between the engineers and the sales executives. Engineers had the firm belief that the hybrid was the answer to all those questions – oil depletion, emissions, and the long-term future of the automobile society – but the businesspeople weren't in agreement. They thought the premium price for a hybrid would make it impossible to sale. Masatami Takimoto, Executive Vice President, sided with the engineers and instructed them to make a concept car with a hybrid powertrain in just 12 months. In addition, he demanded that they raise the fuel-economy target even higher to compensate for higher hybrid costs. To find the right hybrid system for the concept car, now the Prius, the team of engineers went through 80 alternatives before narrowing the list down to four. Once the initial concept was approved, Toyota got serious about putting the Prius into production. The team that was responsible for getting the model into production was given 24 months to develop the car, the hybrid powertrain and everything else, which is about 2/3 the time an automaker would traditionally need to make a conventional vehicle.

Excerpted from, *The Birth of the Prius*
Fortune. March 6, 2006.

What is the relevant business situation facing Toyota?

What are the key skills and competencies employees working on the Prius needed to employ?

Notes:

Mantra to Master

"There is no greater gift you can give or receive than to honor your calling."

Oprah Winfrey

RULE #6:
BE UNDENIABLE

"If someone offers you an amazing opportunity and you're not sure you can do it, say yes – then learn how to do it later."
– Richard Branson

One of the most important things you can do to accelerate your career and set yourself apart is to be undeniable. To be undeniable you need to build a name for yourself as an expert. This is one of the best forms of job security. Not only that, having a standout reputation in a critical niche area can bring with it career advancement and bring you highly sought after promotions. So how do you get those who matter to acknowledge and respond to your expertise?

The key to being undeniable is figuring out what sets you apart from the pack and delivering on that skill again and again. The key is to pick something that has relevance to your company/industry and adds value. When identifying the space, you need to choose a lane that no one else has spotted. It doesn't have to be revolutionary. You don't have to strive necessarily to be the next Steve Jobs. Your expertise might be as simple as being a terrific memo writer or a fast and flawless number cruncher. The goal is that when someone needs the expertise you have your name is top of mind. They know you're the person to call to get the job done, and done well.

Marketing guru, Dorie Clark describes the importance this way in her book *Stand Out: How to Find Your Breakthrough Idea and Build a Following Around It*: "In today's competitive economy, it's not enough to simply do your job well. Developing a reputation as an expert in your field attracts people who want to hire you, do business with you and your company, and spread your ideas. It's the ultimate form of career insurance."

Creating a lane for yourself that has impact across your department or organization allows you to get visibility beyond your cubicle and your boss. When you are known as an expert with a coveted talent other people take notice of you. You start getting the kind of press that makes you, well, undeniable.

If you haven't figured out your expertise don't panic. The great thing about expertise is it can be developed and cultivated. So, if you haven't identified yours there's no time like the present.

Start by looking around your organization to determine who the standouts are in the space that you want to be in? Who do you want to role model? What white space exists? What gaps are currently going unfilled? When you hear people talking, what are the pain points they consistently talk about? What skill or talent could fill that gap?

You also need to stay engaged in your industry. We already talked about the importance of reading and staying abreast of what's happening in your field. It's even more important when you want to carve out a niche for yourself. Staying current on the trends impacting your industry and understanding how those changes apply to your company show a skill and aptitude that demonstrate your value and will have a positive impact on your career growth.

Speak up when your expertise can fill a gap. This is especially important when you're in settings that can be intimidating, like that weekly department meeting the CFO attends. It would be easy to sit there and do your best to try to blend in with the wallpaper. Don't. This is the time, more than ever, when you need to find your voice. The people who make their mark and get ahead don't wait for permission or an invitation to speak—they make sure everyone in the room knows they have something to contribute.

Being undeniable also requires you to think beyond the activity that you are performing to the results you are producing. What does your skill at working with spreadsheets enable the business to accomplish?

Remember, an expert is not perfect. Though this an area that you have staked your claim on you need to be vigilant about staying on top of your game and building your skills in this arena. For this reason, it is crucial to continually seek feedback in the area that you've carved out to ensure you're delivering value. This will also ensure you remain abreast of any changes in the industry or your company that could impact the space you've carved out and equip you to be agile in delivering what your organization needs. This may require you to tweak what, and even how, you're delivering.

NOW, GET TO WORK!

Answer this...

- How can you differentiate yourself from others in your profession?
- Now that you've identified where you'll set yourself apart, what areas do you need to learn more about?
- What opportunities exist for you to distinguish yourself as an expert in the space?

Do this...

- Create a system for debriefing projects that you're on with a focus on growth and development.
- Leave your cubicle! Attend at least two professional workshops or development opportunities this year.
- **Read:** Good to Great by Jim Collins
- **Read:** Patterns of High Performance: Discovering the Ways People Work Best by Jerry Fletcher

Notes:

Life in the
Real World

Role to Master: Leader

The leader seeks to guide or inspire. The leader understands that leadership happens at all levels and does not need to be confined to a title or defined leadership role. The leader is a movie director. Leaders turn a script into a movie; they are responsible for the quality of the final product and its success. Leaders can work with any level of the organization. The leader is adept at communicating the vision and creating a culture where the vision can be executed. The leader guides others to a greater understanding of the strategic motivations and encourages them to perform at a high level. The leader must have the ability to communicate the vision effectively and immediately. The leader must be able to make edits and adjustments when necessary and have a good feel for pacing and structure, integrating people, and distorting resources to ensure things work effectively.

Is this a strength for you? What competencies and skills did you/will you have to develop/use in this role?

Mantra to Master

"The secret of life, though, is to fall seven times and to get up eight times."

Paulo Coelho,
The Alchemist

RULE #7: COMMUNICATE WELL & SPEAK THE LANGUAGE

"Wise men talk because they have something to say; fools, because they have to say something."
– Plato

Effective communication is key to career success. Effective communication has several components. It's a combination of what you say, how you say it, when you say it, and how people feel when you say it.

To be taken seriously, your message, whether verbal or written, needs to be crisp, tight, credible, tailored, and engaging.

Crisp: Despite what you may think, more words don't send a message of more intelligence. A crisp message also allows you to build rapport with your listener by asking what points they need you to expound on.

Tight: Whenever possible practice your message before delivering it. Is your point clear? When you're in a meeting and you don't have time to prepare your message, jot a few bulleted words here and there to keep your message tight. Grammar is also an important component of a tight message. In today's social media era, it's easy to blur the lines between professional and personal. Avoid overly casual and loose communication.

Credible: Do people believe what you've told them? Does your command of the information ring true? In addition, be conscious of words that can detract from your message, such as "um" or "uh" as well as "like" or "so." These words can unintentionally send messages that lack conviction.

Tailored: Understanding your audience is essential to effective communication. Are you communicating to someone who wants quick bullets and one or two options before making a decision? Or does your audience need all the details and plenty of advance notification to mull over a decision before responding? Familiarizing yourself with your audience's needs and preferences is an imperative to communicating well.

Engaging: It's important that people feel your energy, passion and warmth when you are communicating with them. When the communication has concluded, you want them to feel good about themselves, regardless of the message you delivered. This is especially important when you are communicating via e-mail. E-mail communication presents additional challenges because you lose the benefit of seeing people's facial expressions and body language. Additionally, intent has to be inferred when you don't have the ability to communicate face to face or at least over the phone.

Speaking the language means employing the vocabulary of your environment. Every company has a vocabulary all its own. It's the acronyms, words and phrases that relate to the industry and culture of your company. And, it's important that you know yours. For instance, my whole working life I always referred to a PowerPoint presentation as just that or a PowerPoint for short. Well, one day I started with a new company and everyone there kept talking about creating a deck. I had no idea what that was. I chose to smile and nod awkwardly whenever this phantom deck thing was brought up. It was puzzling because everyone seemed to know what this thing was and I felt silly that I didn't. Finally, I mustered up the courage to ask. A deck was simply a printed PowerPoint presentation. The term came about because when printed it resembled a "deck" of cards. That's when I realized the importance of speaking the language. Finally finding my courage to ask the question was timely because later that day my boss asked me to create a deck for an upcoming meeting.

Whew. Crisis averted.

NOW, GET TO WORK!

Do this...

- If you are new to an organization, find out if there is a glossary of commonly used acronyms or words.
- Assess your communication style. Determine what areas you can improve in. Take a course on effective communication or business writing.
- Start reading newspapers, magazines, etc. to increase your ability to contribute to conversations and improve your vocabulary.
- Practice presenting in front of a mirror to assess your nonverbals.
- Take an assessment like DISC to gain insight on your communication preferences.

Notes:

Mantra to Master

"Next time you are afraid to share your idea, remember someone once said in a meeting *'we should make a film about a tornado of sharks'.*"

Unknown

RULE #8:
MASTER THE ART
OF INFLUENCE

"The most common way people give up their power is by thinking they don't have any."
– Alice Walker

An increasing amount of our work these days is done through partnerships with other people. Gone are the days when we could get work done in silos where we had ultimate control. In some ways, this is a good thing. There are more people at the table and people who are impacted by the decisions have more of a voice in the outcomes.

There are also some drawbacks. It takes longer to get things done. When you are the only one who has to say yes, it's a lot quicker than when you must get the buy-in of multiple stakeholders. It also takes more effort. Bicycling around, sharing your ideas with multiple people, and seeking their input takes time...sometimes it takes a lot of time. It can also be frustrating. There are times when you know you have the right idea to fix a broken process, to take an innovative new product to market or to create breakthrough thinking in your company. The problem? No one else knows that you do.

So how do you build the type of influence and power you need to get things done?

First, you need to understand the role of an influencer. Influencers are skilled at directing, persuading, and motivating. Influencers can flex their style to direct, collaborate, or empower, as the situation requires. Influencers have established a personal power base built on mutual trust, fairness, and honesty. Effective influencers persuasively present an educated point of view to influence business decisions. They base their recommendations on sound principles and facts including customer needs, industry trends, and best practices. They influence by presenting implications and recommendations rather than just data and facts. Influencers communicate clearly and concisely while consistently advocating from a customer-centric perspective. They tailor their messages and materials in an audience-appropriate manner.

Next, you need to cast a wide net. Your goal should be to consistently find opportunities to work on meaningful projects with an increasingly expansive group of individuals. Influence is built by having as many people as possible who want you on the team. Your goal is to get to the table. If you aren't at the table you aren't in the conversation. The more tables you are at the greater your power. So, when you aren't present, people will look to invite you to the conversation. "Today's most valuable currency is social capital, defined as the information, expertise, trust, and total value that exist in the relationships you have and social networks to which you belong," explains Keith Ferrazzi, author of *Never Eat Alone: And Other Secrets to Success, One Relationship at a Time.*

Once you've identified the right spaces to be in, you'll need to leverage your expertise. Think about a quarterback at the line of scrimmage. No, think about Peyton Manning at the line of scrimmage. Manning is known for being able to survey how the defense is lining up and based on what he sees changing the play call in the moment. What enables that? It's the expertise he has built. By spending considerable amounts of time playing the game, studying film and learning from his mistakes, Manning knows what matters and what doesn't. He can distinguish between things that are a distraction and what he should give his attention to. He's built a mental muscle that allows him to confidently and, more importantly, consistently make winning decisions. Manning does what Charles Duhigg describes in *The Power of Habit* "Champions don't do extraordinary things. They do ordinary things, but they do them without thinking, too fast for the other team to react. They follow the habits they've learned."

NOW, GET TO WORK!

Do this...

- Read: *Influence: The Psychology of Persuasion* by Robert B. Cialdini
- Identify someone with exceptional influence skills. Observe how he or she works. Identify 2-3 skills this person employs that you want to practice.

Notes:

Life in the
Real World

Role to Master: Assimilator

The assimilator endeavors to adapt to the environment. The assimilator understands the culture, customs, language, and survival mechanisms of the organization and leverages that understanding to ensure success. The assimilator studies normal social behaviors and how certain factors influence deviation from that norm. The assimilator examines the relationship between the environment and actions that affect it. The assimilator is a politician who is organizationally astute and culturally savvy. Often the most difficult role to navigate, the successful assimilator knows how to be in the organization, but not of the organization. The assimilator understands there various and disparate constituencies that contribute to success.

Is this a strength for you? What competencies and skills did you/will you have to develop/ use in this role?

Mantra to Master

"Nobody is gonna hit as hard as life, but it ain't how hard you can hit. It's how hard you can get hit and keep moving forward. It's how much you can take, and keep moving forward. That's how winning is done."

Rocky, from Rocky Balboa

RULE #9:
LEARN TO GIVE &
RECEIVE FEEDBACK

"There is only one way to avoid criticism: do nothing, say nothing, and be nothing."
– Aristotle

Successful people are successful because they are unwaveringly focused on constantly getting better. To do that they need to be aware of what they do well and conscious of where their blind spots are. The only way to do this is to be relentless about getting feedback. This takes some practice because receiving feedback that isn't positive and affirming can be challenging to stomach.

In his book, *The Power of Choice*, Michael Hyter tells a great story about how early in his career he approached a senior leader to get constructive feedback that would support his growth and development. He was used to hearing that he was doing a great job, yet he was not advancing in the way he had hoped. He was sure there was something more he needed to hear. In his next meeting with his boss, he tried again to get the feedback that he needed. The leader started by giving him the same meaningless platitudes that he had already heard. Intent on getting better, Hyter decided to use a different approach. He gave the executive permission to be candid. As Hyter notes, "...when you send a strong message that you want direct feedback, and when you're willing to make the person providing the feedback feel safe giving it to you, you make yourself "feedback worthy." In return, you're likely to get invaluable information that will accelerate your growth."

So how do you position yourself in such a way to, as Hyter calls it, make yourself "feedback worthy?" Start by having an out of body experience of sorts. Simply put, don't take the feedback personal. Whenever you are getting feedback try this: You are a researcher who has been given the assignment of translating the information to be shared. See the feedback as data you need to collect to help you make the project, in this case, you, even better. By stepping outside of yourself to hear the feedback, no matter what you hear, positive or negative, you can manage it. Great feedback won't lull you into complacency and difficult or bad feedback won't become paralyzing.

Next, learn to keep the meat and discard the bones. Everyone who provides you feedback won't have your best interest in mind. In addition, not everyone who gives you feedback will know how to do so in a manner that is useful. For both reasons, you need to get good at mentally sifting through the feedback you receive. Ask yourself:
- Is this feedback actionable?
- Ego aside, is there anything in this feedback that might be even remotely true?

- If I do something with this information what will be the impact? Will I get better at something that matters?

If the answer to these questions is no, thank the person for sharing and keep it moving.

Third, create an action plan to address the feedback. Prioritize the actions you'll take. Figure out a timeline based on what needs to be implemented sooner rather than later. Then determine appropriate deadlines. Be sure to measure your success and share your progress. Most companies have a standard individual development plan (IDP) template, that would serve as the perfect vehicle for you to use for this exercise.

To demonstrate your ability to handle feedback you must be willing to listen without interjecting or making excuses. You should avoid pointing the finger or blaming others. You'll want to demonstrate curiosity by asking questions for clarity. Finally, you'll have to demonstrate your willingness to change the behavior by being solution-oriented and identifying real actions to get better. The ability to accept feedback and create positive actions to improve is a key skill for successful professionals. Your willingness to do so will telegraph to your manager and other executives that you are interested in getting better and that you have the right level of emotional intelligence to accept feedback with the right balance of grace and humility.

Now that you've mastered receiving feedback, you want to be sure that you also give great feedback. Be sure the feedback you give is clear, concrete, actionable, and has meaning to the receiver. You'll also want to be sure that you are focused on behaviors and have specific examples to share. Lastly, be sure to praise in public and correct in private. Remember, the goal of giving others feedback should be based on a genuine interest in seeing them get better or improving a project/process. If the feedback you're offering isn't based on that fundamental idea and doesn't serve that purpose, keep it to yourself.

"Most of us avoid telling the truth because it's uncomfortable. We're afraid of the consequences—making others feel uncomfortable, hurting their feelings, or risking their anger. And yet, when we don't tell the truth, and others don't tell us the truth, we can't deal with matters from a basis in reality. We've all heard the phrase that "the truth will set you free." And it will. The truth allows us to be free to deal with the way things are, not the way we imagine them to be or hope them to be or might manipulate them to be with our lies. The truth also frees up our energy. It takes energy to withhold the truth, keep a secret, or keep up an act." — Jack Canfield, *The Success Principles: How to Get from Where You Are to Where You Want to Be*

NOW, GET TO WORK!

Do this...
- Read: *Crucial Conversations by Kerry Patterson.*
- Practice with a trusted colleague.

Notes:

Mantra to Master

"When you find your path, you must not be afraid. You need to have sufficient courage to make mistakes. Disappointment, defeat, and despair are the tools God uses to show us the way."

Paulo Coelho,
Brida

Life in the
Real World

Skill to Develop: Problem-solving & Creative Thinking

A company's ability to achieve its strategic objectives often depends on how quickly and effectively it can transcend barriers to improved productivity and competitiveness. These pressures put problem solving and creative thinking at a premium — at all levels of an organization.

Problem solving includes the ability to recognize and define problems, invent and implement solutions, and track and evaluate results. New approaches to problem solving, organizational design, or product development all spring from the individual capacity for creative thinking.

Is this a strength for you? What competencies and skills did you/will you have to develop/use in this role?

RULE #10: MANAGE YOUR BOSS

"If you don't design your own life plan, chances are you'll fall into someone else's plan. And guess what they have planned for you? Not much."
- **Jim Rohn**

Once upon a time in a faraway land lived a man named John. John worked hard but, despite how much he wanted to, he couldn't get along with his boss. John just didn't like his boss. He didn't respect his boss. In all honesty, John couldn't stand the very sound of his boss' voice. Before long John was unemployed. The End.

Too dramatic? Ok, I'll give you that. But, you get the general idea. If you can't get along with your boss, it won't be long before you'll be looking for your next opportunity. No matter how incompetent, distant, unsupportive, etc. you perceive your boss to be, it is your job to figure out how to build a bridge and form a productive relationship with him or her. On the other hand, maybe your boss isn't any of those things but you're just unsure of how to build rapport.

The first thing to remember is that you are not in competition with your boss. While you may aspire to achieve the level of success your boss has, your relationship doesn't have to be a rivalry for you to do so. The fact that your boss is in the position she is in means there are things you can learn from her, such as how she got to where she is in her career. Ultimately, you need to see your boss as a resource who can:

- Help you navigate the sometimes-political waters of the organization.
- Secure the resources you need to make your project a success.
- Advocate for you on interdepartmental issues.
- Champion you for promotions and during succession planning discussion.

So how do you get your boss to be willing to stick her neck out for you? How do you get her to stake her personal reputation and credibility on your success.

You start by differentiating yourself with your boss. You can do this by giving her something she needs, but currently lacks. "Star performers are very likely to attract sponsors, and loyal performers are very likely to keep them. But if they fail to distinguish themselves, these loyal performers run the risk of becoming permanent seconds, lieutenants who never make captain. To position themselves for the top job, protégés must therefore contribute something the leader prizes but may intrinsically lack," Sylvia Ann Hewlett notes in *Forget a Mentor, Find a Sponsor: The New Way to Fast-Track Your Career*.

You should also:

Over-communicate. The last thing your boss wants is to be caught off-guard or surprised in a meeting with her boss or peers. This doesn't mean that you need to provide your boss with a detailed account of how you spend every day. Rather, what you want to do is align early on the types of issues or situations your boss wants to be looped in on. While you're at it, find out how your boss wants to be notified. Does she prefer a quick text message or phone call, or does she want to see the whites of your eyes?

Meet the deadline. If your boss asks you to get something submitted on Friday, you do not want her to come looking for it on Monday. When this happens, it starts to erode trust. You never know who your boss has set expectations with to have the project done by a designated, predetermined date. When you are late it has potential ramifications beyond the immediate situation you are privy to. Make it a rule of thumb that when you commit to an assignment, you'll be maniacal about hitting the deadline.

Be honest. Be clear about how you like to work, where you are on the big project, when you don't know the answer, when you're overwhelmed, and even when your boss is about to make a mistake.

Be curious. There are times when your interaction with your boss might leave you scratching your head, wondering if this person is invested in your success. With so much happening around us, it is easy to begin telling ourselves stories that attempt to make sense of seemingly illogical moments. Your boss gives your co-worker the plum project to work on. Or your boss appears to dismiss your idea without hearing you out. These or other similar situations occur and you create a story about why. Generally, your boss is cast as the bad guy and you as the long-suffering victim in the story. Are these stories true? "...Just after we observe what others do and just before we feel some emotion about it, we tell ourselves a story. We add meaning to the action we observed. We make a guess at the motive driving the behavior. Why were they doing that? We also add judgment—is that good or bad? And then, based on these thoughts or stories, our body responds with an emotion," Kerry Patterson, *Crucial Conversations Tools for Talking When Stakes Are High*.

Rather than creating conspiracy theories, the better response in that moment is for you to slow down and get curious. Ask questions to understand what happened. "In fact, with experience and maturity we learn to worry less about others' intent and more about the effect others' actions are having on us. No longer are we in the game of rooting out unhealthy motives. Here is the good news. When we reflect on alternative motives, not only do we soften our emotions, but equally important, we relax our absolute certainty long enough to allow for dialogue— the only reliable way of discovering others' genuine motives advises Patterson, *Crucial Conversations*.

Being curious allows you to stay engaged instead of sulking or nursing your wounds. Demonstrating positive curiosity - asking questions in a way that adds value - also shows your emotional intelligence. A great way of illustrating this concept comes from a conversation I had a few years ago with Audra Bohannon, a leadership consultant and Senior Partner with Korn/Ferry International. Bohannon says in every situation what determines the outcome is our reaction to a situation not the situation itself. In a nutshell, "it's not the stimulus, it's the response."

To effectively manage your boss you must decide to do everything in your power to make your boss successful. This means you'll have to spend time understanding who your boss is, what makes her tick, and what her career ambitions are. You'll also want to discover her idiosyncrasies, those things that make her start twitching, like self-promoters, complainers, people who don't speak up in meetings, and anyone who roots for the Lakers. Once you are clear on what they are, you will know never to do any of them. The optimal boss-subordinate relationship is a true quid pro quo relationship, this for that. The more success you create for your boss the more chances, in the way of special projects, assignments, etc., she'll be willing to give you to do just that.

There are times when, despite all the managing up you do, your boss is unbearable. Remember the situation our friend Peter is trying to navigate through? Trying to figure out what to do when despite your best efforts every single day you go to work for Attila the Hun incarnate? It might be time to contemplate a career change.

NOW, GET TO WORK!

Do this...

- Invite your boss out for coffee/lunch. Spend the time getting to know her better. Identify at least one thing that you can learn from her.
- Find out your boss' key priorities. Identify at least one that you can help him accomplish. Remember to over deliver.
- Read: *The Power of Choice* by Michael Hyter

Notes:

Mantra to Master

"It takes 20 years to build a reputation and five minutes to ruin it. If you think about that, you'll do things differently."

Warren Buffet

RULE #11: EXPAND YOUR CIRCLE

"Relationships are all there is. Everything in the universe only exists because it is in relationship to everything else. Nothing exists in isolation. We have to stop pretending we are individuals that can go it alone."

- Margaret Wheatley

Relationships are the linchpin of success these days. No one gets anything done alone and no one finds success if they can't work well with others. This means that you need to be adept at building relationships.

Think about the best relationships you have. Great relationships are rarely about what others do, but more about how they make us feel. That idea holds true about our working relationships too. The goal isn't about making everyone your best friend, but it is about building meaningful, authentic relationships that are not only mutually beneficially but can also serve as a support system on those challenging days. Here's how:

Be willing to fall on the sword. Sometimes you have to take one for the team. The group presentation bombed. The customer didn't get the order on time. Everyone took an early Friday and your boss needs help getting ready for a big Monday meeting. There are times when you have more political capital saved up than someone else and for that reason you can take the hit. People will remember your selflessness.

Don't wait to be asked. Your co-worker in the cubicle next to you is drowning. He's been in the office after 7pm every night for the last two weeks. When you passed him earlier in the hallway coming from the restroom your eyes briefly met and you could have sworn there were tears in his eyes. He said it was because the Knicks lost, but secretly you're not sure. His pride has clearly gotten the best of him. Instead of waiting to see if he'll ask for your help, just give it. Do it in a completely unobtrusive way that will assure him you aren't looking too steal his shine.

Offer solutions. You know what every company has no shortage of? Problems. They are lying around every corner waiting to pounce. The problem, no pun intended, is that few people have solutions to go along with them. People who bring solutions, who solve people's problems, are prized among their peers.

Occasionally be a shrinking violet. Sometimes it's not your turn. Sometimes it's ok to let someone else have their moment. Be generous with your praise and appreciation of others. Find opportunities to help others accomplish their goals. As Ferrazzi says in the best-selling, *Never Eat Alone: And Other Secrets to Success, One Relationship at a Time,* "Connecting. It's a constant process of giving and receiving—of asking for and offering help. By putting people in contact with one another, by giving your time and expertise and sharing them freely, the pie gets bigger for everyone. This karma-tinged vision of how things work may sound naïve to those who have grown cynical of the business world. But while the power of generosity is not yet fully appreciated, or applied, in the halls of corporate America, its value in the world of networks is proven."

Hear everyone. Have you ever been in one of those meetings where one person says something and no one notices, then five seconds later someone else says the same thing and people respond as if they'd heard it for the first time? Don't be one of those people. Great ideas can come from anywhere. Building great relationships is about knowing when you've heard something powerful, impactful, or transformational and being able to give it the credit it deserves, regardless of the source.

Be vulnerable. Sometimes it's just not your day. Sometimes your best isn't good enough. Sometimes you drop the ball. Sometimes it really is your fault. For some the natural reaction in those moments is to make excuses, to CYB (cover your butt), to point the finger elsewhere. Why do we do this? We do it because work can be a scary place. We think we'll get fired, we think we'll have a scarlet letter painted on our chest, we think we'll be burned at the stake. Resist the urge. Instead, be willing to be vulnerable. Acknowledge your mistake. If necessary, apologize. People who are willing to own their mistakes have little difficulty building powerful relationships.

My friend, Alan, who is the Vice President, Global Diversity & Inclusion for a leading global biotechnology company, is exceptionally talented at building and nurturing relationships. In fact, he creates a relationship map and identifies who he has key relationships with and what he needs from each. By defining expected outcomes, he can specifically identify what he needs to do to obtain the result he desires. Here is his model:

Andrea Ambition Relationship Map

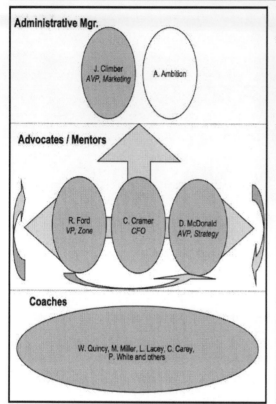

Role	Expected Outcome
Ensure Alignment, Clarity, Proactive Steps	" She can do it..." " I stake my personal reputation and credibility on her success..."
Provide actionable, specific feedback (brutal facts, both good and bad) Actively communicate with one another	" I've really been impressed with what Andrea brings to the table...haven't you?" " We have to find a place for Andrea in the future state of the enterprise..." " She has continued to mature as a leader and has taken complete accountability for her growth and development..."
Provide informal coaching and feedback, serve as a sounding board, provide additional networking opportunities	" Andrea has a well thought-out plan and is successfully executing against it..."

Administrative Mgr.

J. Climber
AVP, Marketing

A. Ambition

Advocates / Mentors

R. Ford
VP, Zone

C. Cramer
CFO

D. McDonald
AVP, Strategy

Coaches

W. Quincy, M. Miller, L. Lacey, C. Carey, P. White and others

NOW, GET TO WORK!

Do this...

- Build a relationship map. Create a strategy for how you'll invest in and develop each of these relationships.
- Ask for a skip level meeting with your boss' boss.
- Every quarter identify 2 or 3 people within your organization or industry that you would like to know better. Reach out and invite them for coffee or lunch.
- Constantly nurture your network. Don't wait until you need something. Check in with people. See how they're doing. Listen for cues on ways you can add value or help them.
- **Read:** *Who's Got Your Back: The Breakthrough Program to Build Deep, Trusting Relationships That Create Success--And Won't Let You Fail* by Keith Ferrazzi

Notes:

PETER'S PROBLEM

Let's revisit Peter who we met earlier. Peter was working in his dream job where he had the benefit of doing cutting edge work, the very work he has spent his life preparing for. Recently Peter's boss left the organization and now he has a new boss. This is his new boss' first time leading a team. Additionally, he does not have the educational background that Peter has. In Peter's estimation, his boss does not understand the foundational issues of the work they need to accomplish. Peter believes his boss' tactical manner is not only unfitting of someone in a leadership position but it is also unfocused, counter-productive, and ineffective, leading to what Peter believes are some very costly errors. All of this is causing Peter great difficulty.

Peter is contemplating whether he should have ever left academia. Is his relationship with his boss really going to derail Peter's career and cost him his opportunity to make an impact?

Based on what you have read so far, what advice would you give Peter?

Life in the
Real World

Role to Master: Observer

The observer's primary goal is to build awareness. The observer is watching without judging or drawing conclusions. The observer watches how and why things happen. The observer is a detective who gathers information. The observer looks for gaps in the evidence and obstacles impacting the execution of strategy. The observer sees, hears, or in some other way notices what's going on in the world and becomes curious about what's happening. The observer notices something, and wonders why it happens. The observer sees something and wonders what causes it.

The first step of observation is to clear the mind of any preconceived judgments. Note taking is critical to the observation process. Writing down what happens ensures that nothing is missed or forgotten.

Is this a strength for you? What competencies and skills did you/will you have to develop/use in this role?

Mantra to Master

"Even if you haven't quite figured out HOW it's all going to work and if it's ever going to happen, DO it anyway. Keep reminding yourself to move your dreams from your head and into the universe. You'll be surprised at how much you actually accomplish."

Myleik Teele, *CEO, Curlbox*

RULE #12: SURPASS YOUR LIMITS

"I realized that despite the fear and the bruises of life, one has to keep on fighting for one's dream. And one has to understand that braveness is not the absence of fear but rather the strength to keep on going forward despite the fear."
- Paulo Coelho

I have a coaching client, Marcus, whose favorite two phrases are, «But, what if...» or «I can't, because...» The sentiment underlying both phrases is fear. He's afraid to make a mistake, big or small. He's afraid to take risks, even when his boss encourages him to do so, he's concerned that maybe he's being set-up to fail. He's afraid that his job is on the line with every project he undertakes. Every day he walks on eggshells attempting to navigate a minefield of «what if's» and boogie men around every corner.

The problem is that Marcus' fears are all in his head. His boss and the other executives Marcus works with think very highly of him. They've identifies him as a Hi-Po and they are even investing in his development by allowing him to work with a Leadership Coach (yours truly) and other investments in his development. They've seen his hard work and believe he has a future with the organization. However, his inability to move beyond this seemingly irrational fear is starting to cause a concern and create a question. They question it creates is, how will he respond at the next level when or now if he's given more responsibility?

Marcus understands that failing to get his fear under control and allowing it to drive his decision making is having a harmful impact on his ongoing career success. By playing it safe, he's missing out on opportunities to continue to grow. His anxiety is impeding his ability to get new, high value projects, try new things and ultimately his ability to develop new skills.

If you're in a similar place to Marcus, you'll benefit from approaching your situation in the same manner I suggested to him. We've all read those stories of people who, when confronted with scary situations, somehow tapped into superhuman strength to save a child from an angry bear or lift a car to secure someone's safety. What those moments illustrate is that when the conditions are right and you put your mind to it there's really nothing you can't do.

So how do you recreate similar adrenaline pumping moments at your 9 to 5? Well, it's not as hard as you might think.

Know the why as much as the how. Start by understanding the why of what you do. It's easy to get really focused on executing. We have a million to dos and we want to move through our list quickly. However, in our quest to be efficient we fail to truly grasp the real why of the work we are tasked with. Why does the process work the way it does? Understanding why allows you to get clear on what the real answer to the problem is. Furthermore, it allows you to fix and adjust as challenges arise.

"A person who knows how may always have a job, but the person who knows why will always be his boss," John C. Maxwell, *How Successful People Think: Change Your Thinking, Change Your Life.*

To do this you should employ a childlike curiosity. Children ask a million questions. Chief among them is why. They continue to ask why until the adults around them grow exasperated. But, this doesn't thwart their inquisitiveness. The next time they have a question it's back to the why game. Something happens, however, as we get older. First in school then at work we become socialized into believing that there is no reward for asking questions. There is no value in spending time to understand the problem at hand. We learn that the prize goes to those who produce quick solutions.

To shift this paradigm, try a new approach. The next time you're working on something, rather than rotely going through the motions, pause and ask questions to understand why:

- What problem are you trying to solve?
- How does this connect to the organization strategy?
- What situation(s) led to this task?
- Where did the original idea come from?
- Who will benefit from it?
- What would happen if it weren't done?
- What pain points exist in completing the task?
- How do you know when it's been done well?

Take notes. Another essential strategy in surpassing your limits is to put pen to paper. If you are anything like me, your mind is constantly going. Ideas flow like an open fire hydrant on a hot day. The problem is sometimes the ideas come at moments when I can't do anything with them: on the bus, in the shower, in the middle of a pedicure you get the idea. And, invariably, by the time I get around to writing the idea down, it's gone. Lost in the dark void where great ideas go to disappear. Now maybe you don't always have access to pen and paper, but you probably do have access to the next best thing, your cell phone. Record a memo to yourself, use the notes section or send yourself an email. This will ensure that all those great ideas don't get lost.

Finish. One of my favorite things to do is to go for a nice brisk run. When I can I like to get in four to five miles. Those runs are especially wonderful when I hit the zone. That wonderful place where you literally feel like you could run for hours without tiring or losing your pace. I love the zone. Unfortunately, I don't hit it every time I lace up my sneakers. On those days when the zone is elusive it's a chore to push myself to the finish.

It's not only during a run when finishing can be tough. Even at work many of us start well but we sputter out when it's time to finish. The tension is between our motivation and execution. Newness is shiny and sexy. However, when banality of the day to day monotony of the project or tasks sets in, finding the motivation to move forward becomes arduous, so we put on the brakes. Sometimes we feel overwhelmed because we discover we're in over our heads and with that discouragement comes a larger fear of failure.

To overcome this paralysis try keeping a journal of completed projects to remind yourself of your contributions and accomplishments. Also, stop getting stuck on the big picture. You know what you need to do. Now break it down into manageable pieces so you can get it done. And stop waiting until the last minute. People often brag about working best under pressure. This is rarely the case. Imagine if Olympic athlete approached their task in such a cavalier way. Do you think they would be successful, cramming the night before a big race? Yeah, I think we both know the answer to that one.

Establish milestones. Now you need to set some mile markers for yourself, reasonable benchmarks to let you know you're making progress. The prospect of surpassing your limits may seem daunting but, to continue propelling yourself forward, especially in those difficult moments, you must take time to acknowledge and celebrate your achievements, big and small. Establish small tasks and set individual success metrics to keep yourself motivated and your efficacy high. Share your accomplishments as appropriate, document your progress and reward yourself.

Eliminate fear. Sometimes the biggest thing that stands in our way of doing more is the story we've told ourselves about why we can't. We're not smart enough. We don't have the right pedigree. So, tell yourself a new story. What if you are a brilliant, talented, articulate communicator who delivers kick-ass presentations? And, then what if you go in there and do just that? I don't know, call me crazy, you might become a legend. The company rock star. It could happen.

"One good thing about aspiration is that it's quite easy to tell whether or not you have it." If you're not actually taking steps to do something, then you don't really want to do it, no matter what you're telling yourself. Your aspiration is insufficient. Period," Erika Andersen, *Be Bad First: Get Good at Things Fast to Stay Ready for the Future.*

Stand shoulder to shoulder with your anxiety. Ok, you tried the new story and that didn't work? Then play the fear out to the end. Scared of that big presentation you have to deliver? What's the worst that could happen? You forget your lines? Use notes. You'll faint? Have someone with smelling salts on standby. Someone will ask you a question you don't have an answer for? Research as much as you can and if they still throw you a stumper be honest and tell them you'll follow up. The point here is that nothing is insurmountable.

Shonda Rhimes has the best advice for getting through this moment, in her book *Year of Yes: How to Dance It Out, Stand In the Sun and Be Your Own Person*, "Who you are today . . . that's who you are. Be brave. Be amazing. Be worthy. And every single time you get the chance? Stand up in front of people. Let them see you. Speak. Be heard. Go ahead and have the dry mouth. Let your heart beat so, so fast. Watch everything move in slow motion. So, what. You what? You pass out, you die, you poop? No."

Create a visual. Grab a sheet of paper and draw a box in the center. The box represents your comfort zone. Inside the box write 10-15 things that you're really good at, you like doing, or that you're comfortable doing. Outside the box identify 10-15 things that create some level of discomfort. Give yourself a range of things, from those that are benign to those that will get your heart racing but if done will also have a big reward. Periodically choose something from the list outside the box to help you get comfortable surpassing your limits.

Make sure you have a support system. Having people to encourage you through the process and celebrate with you in the end will make the process of taking risks and pushing yourself less intimidating.

NOW, GET TO WORK!

Do this...

- Identify an area where you could go harder than you are currently. What's holding you back? What would be the result if you pushed past that barrier? What support do you need to do so?

Notes:

Mantra to Master

"If you obsess over whether you are making the right decision, you are basically assuming that the universe will reward you for one thing and punish you for another. The universe has no fixed agenda. Once you make any decision, it works around that decision."

Deepak Chopra

RULE #13: BEWARE THE SHINY PENNY

"The only thing that I see that is distinctly different about me is I'm not afraid to die on a treadmill. I will not be out-worked, period. You might have more talent than me, you might be smarter than me, you might be sexier than me, you might be all of those things you got it on me in nine categories. But if we get on the treadmill together, there's two things: You're getting off first, or I'm going to die. It's really that simple, right?"
- Will Smith

I have a secret to share with you. I'm drawn to distractions. I know I'm not alone. You love them too. At least that's what the latest research on productivity and focus suggests. According to a recent article in *Forbes* magazine, we are just like monkeys in that we get a shot of dopamine every time something pulls us in another direction. You still think it's a bunch of malarkey? The researchers suggest asking yourself why you check your email so often.

According to these same researchers, making lists and downing double espressos isn't going to get us any closer to the productivity and focus we desire. We have to first get clear about what true productivity is. It isn't checking off tasks from your overwhelming to do list. In our quest for the euphoric feeling that a productive day induces we get caught in the deception that making lists will lead us there. It won't. Accomplishing a bunch of things isn't productivity. Instead, we need to think of productivity in the same way most highly successful people do. Rather than trying to do more things, make a point to do more of the right things. In a nutshell, like any good poker player, you need to focus on your blue chips, those things that, when done well, will have the highest value.

How you ask?

Stop multitasking. Doing a million things at once creates the "illusion" of productivity. There's a natural high that comes from moving at lightning speed through a lengthy to do list. But it's just that, an illusion. According to research, switching from task to task quickly does not work. When you multitask, your IQ actually drops by an average of 10 points. (For men, the drop is 15 points and five for women.) As your IQ drops you become more prone to mistakes. Or as productivity expert Julie Morgenstern notes, "...studies have shown that we have a much lower retention rate of what we learn when multitasking, which means you could have to redo the work or you may not do the next task well because you forgot the information you learned."

Remember that perfection is the enemy of good enough. Everyone wants to do great work. However, sometimes that desire can be paralyzing. As Dr. Alex Lickerman notes in a 2011 article in *Psychology Today*, "At some point, we must remind ourselves, any changes we make to a creation no longer make it better but just different (and sometimes worse)." Or as Jon Acuff notes in *Quitter*, "90 percent perfect and shared with the world always changes more lives than 100 percent perfect and stuck in your head." So how can we break free from this sometimes debilitating habit?

Replace perfection with a drive for excellence. Get a vision for what perfect looks like and what good enough looks like. For example, when I ran my first half marathon perfect would have been channeling my inner Kenyan and killing the race in a Boston marathon qualifying time. However, since it was my first race, I was beyond ecstatic when I ran the entire race and finished in a better time than in all my training runs.

Follow the 80/20 rule. Think about the end of a typical workday. When you're packing up your stuff getting ready to head out of the door how do you normally feel? Do you have a sense of accomplishment? Can you look back on the day and identify where you had the greatest impact? Or is it the opposite. When you do a mental scan of your day do you look back only to feel as if the entire day slipped through your fingers? Do you have a difficult time identifying what, if anything, you actually did? Well, if your life feels more like the latter, then Houston we have a problem.

With so much coming at us it's easy to end up with more days where we accomplish someone else's to do list rather than our own. However, that doesn't have to be the case. By applying the 80/20 rule you can accomplish the things that matter most and have the greatest impact on your success. In a nutshell, the 80/20 rule states that only 20 percent of what you do each day produces 80 percent of your results.

What this means is that you can be more effective if you figure out how to eliminate the things that don't matter during your workday because they have a minimal effect on your overall productivity. You're probably thinking, "I can't possibly eliminate anything that I do, everything is important." There's probably more that you can get rid of than you think.

Be really interested in what matters to your boss. As Mihaly Csikszentmihalyi says in *Flow: The Psychology Of Engagement With Every day Life*, "If you are interested in something, you will focus on it, and if you focus attention on anything, it is likely that you will become interested in it. Many of the things we find interesting are not so by nature, but because we took the trouble of paying attention to them."

Think about the feedback you receive. What things get your boss' attention? What things seem to matter most to your boss? Scan the priorities for your week ahead. Of all the things you have to accomplish, which, if done well, will generate the biggest return for your organization? When you have the answer to those questions, do those things.

Don't be afraid to say no, but do so sparingly. Using the word no, is one of the most intimidating things to do at work. It feels like you aren't being a team player. You're worried that if you say no this time, you may not get a chance to say yes next time. Still, it's important to value your time and choose your yeses wisely. Of course, this is easier when you've built a record of success. If this is your first job or you're new to an organization it may be harder to say no. Try the strategy Stephen Covey outlined in his best-selling *Seven Habits of Highly Effective People*, "You have to decide what your highest priorities are and have the courage—pleasantly, smilingly, nonapologetically, to say 'no' to other things. And the way you do that is by having a bigger "yes" burning inside. The enemy of the "best" is often the "good."

Plan your day. Meetings consume a significant portion of our day. That means we have to be very conscious of how we organize our day to ensure we are getting the most out of it. If the majority of your day is being spent in meetings you have to be disciplined about how you spend the time you do have at your desk. It's so easy to spend that 20-minute break between meetings trying to provide short responses to an inbox full of emails. Is that really the best use of your time or should you, instead, finish pulling together the draft memo announcing the department restructuring for your manager's review? Those emails seem so easy that you convince yourself responding to them will be the better choice. You'll get them out of the way and then get to what matters. Problem is the easy stuff keeps piling up. When you finally get around to the memo, you're so busy rushing to meet the deadline that it gets short shrift. You may even get it in by the deadline but is it really the best representation of you?

NOW, GET TO WORK!

Do this...

- Figure out what matters the most. What are the things you work on that yield the greatest return? Make sure your time and energy are distorted to those things.
- **Read:** *Focus: The Hidden Driver of Excellence* by Daniel Goleman
- **Read:** *Ready for Anything: 52 Productivity Principles for Getting Things Done* by David Allen

Notes:

Mantra to Master

"Hey! I'm a keep running. Because a winner don't quit on themselves."

Beyonce,
Freedom

RULE #14: DON'T LET IDIOTS RUIN YOUR DAY

"When they go low; we go high."
- **First Lady Michelle Obama**

We all know them. Every office has one or two. Those people who like to be in the middle of drama, get things done with a bulldozer, always go from 0 to 100 unprovoked or are just generally toxic people. There is an art to managing those types of individuals without turning into a terror yourself and learning how is a must.

For starters, quit allowing these people into your head. This requires real skill. Allowing yourself to be consumed by someone else's actions or constantly ruminating on what someone else is thinking will only undermine your own efforts. You constantly play tapes in your mind of how they'll respond or react to every situation. You contemplate their feedback before you've ever heard it. They own you.

Now, strip them of their power. The last thing you want to do is allow toxic people to control your mood and your experience at work. To the best of your ability take the emotion out of your encounters with them. Ultimately, it's not personal. I remember working with someone like this and, honestly, it was exhausting to constantly think about what this person was going to do or say next. Until I decided that, despite how annoying it was, I couldn't control this person, but I could control my response to the behavior.

There will come a time when you'll be having a bad day and this person will provide a willing ear for some good old-fashioned negative bonding. You'll be tempted to give in just this one time. The processes are flawed. The boss is MIA. No one is carrying their own weight. You'll want to vent. You'll need to vent. Don't. If you crack open the door, even a little, they will feel that they have found an ally in their negativity, and every time they need to let lose they'll come looking for you.

It's also important that you set boundaries, respectfully. Maybe the person you have to deal with likes to gossip or has an abusive communication style. Whatever the challenge, pull him or her to the side in a neutral environment and explain your concerns. When you do broach the subject do so in a non-accusatory but direct manner.

Don't let someone steal your happiness. Surround yourself with positive people. Don't replay every encounter you've had with the toxic person when you're with others. Focus on solutions not problems. People will be watching how you handle the situation. You want them to see you operating in an emotionally intelligent manner.

"We — not our company — are responsible for our attitudes. What happens each day at work doesn't get to determine my attitude, I do. Attitude is a decision. And it's a decision we have to make every day, sometimes every hour if that particular day is especially whack," Jon Acuff, *Do Over: Rescue Monday, Reinvent Your Work, and Never Get Stuck*

Your best secret weapon is a positive attitude. This means, no matter what is happening on a project, maintain a cheerful attitude at all times. Remaining optimistic and upbeat in the face of negativity is a true skill. At first you won't feel it, but do it anyway. As the saying goes, fake it until you make it. All it takes is a few days of smiling when you don't feel like it and you will start a cycle going that will make you feel better all the time.

When people see you as someone cheerful and positive, that telegraphs a message that you don't have time for shenanigans. You'll be a magnet for other positive folks and negative folks will know to get on the bandwagon or keep their distance.

NOW, GET TO WORK!

Do this...

- **Read:** *Crucial Accountability: Tools for Resolving Violated Expectations, Broken Commitments, and Bad Behavior* by Kerry Patterson, Joseph Grenny, Ron McMillan
- **Read:** *Boundaries: When to Say Yes, How to Say No to Take Control of Your Life* by Henry Cloud

Notes:

Life in the
Real World

Skill to Develop: Managing Self

The ability to take responsibility for one's own performance, including the awareness, development and application of one's own skills and competencies.

The ability to control one's own behavior and improve one's own performance, recognizing and overcoming barriers along the way. Being aware of one's self and surroundings, being able to lead oneself and manage one's career. Being able to handle and adapt to changing, ambiguous and often conflicting circumstances in the immediate environment.

What it looks like:

*   Don't wait for your manager to tell you what you need to know to do your job;
*   Proactively seek development opportunities.
*   Assess and define problems you are facing;
*   Develop a plan for achieving your goals;
*   Determine whether the plan is working and revise where necessary.

Is this a strength for you? What competencies and skills did you/will you have to develop/ use in this role?

NICOLE'S ANXIETY

Remember Nicole? She was the banking executive who left a cushy job that she knew well for an opportunity in a new and unfamiliar industry because it paid significantly more than she was previously making. She was feeling a great deal of anxiety because, even though she felt like her new company was a great place to work, she was concerned that their expectations were unrealistic and she would be unable to fulfill them. She had been hired to facilitate training on a software platform, known as SAP. She had never utilized SAP before and felt like she shouldn't be expected to grasp the material and be an expert in only eight weeks' time.

She was starting to question if her decision to leave an environment that she knew so well and where she was on the fast track was the right decision. She was still in her probationary period.

What if they decided they had made the wrong decision?

Based on what you have read so far, what advice would you give Nicole?

Mantra to Master

"On this day 18 years ago the Hornets told me right after they drafted me that they had no use for me and were going to trade me."

Kobe Bryant, retired NBA 4 time MVP, 18 time all-star, 5-time league champion

RULE #15: IT'S OKAY TO LEAVE

"You are responsible for your life. If you're sitting around waiting on somebody to save you, to fix you, to even help you, you are wasting your time. Only you have the power to move your life forward."
- Oprah Winfrey

There are certain companies that everyone dreams of working in. So much so that if you work there and decide to leave people look at you as if you must have had a mental break. The thing is, there's always life after Apple, Nike, Starbucks, Google, you fill in the blank.

Despite that declaration, I know firsthand, making the decision to leave your current employer is still a scary decision. Even so, sometimes that is the decision you have to make. So how do you know when it's time to go?

- **Despite your best efforts, you and your boss can't get on the same page.** Your direct manager is the single biggest determiner of job satisfaction and career advancement. If your boss is incompetent, unsupportive, toxic or all of the above, cut your losses now.

- **You're not advancing or developing**. Getting passed over for a promotion isn't reason enough to leave. Sometimes it's an opportunity to learn and further refine your skills. Yet, sometimes a lack of advancement is the perfect sign that it's time to explore other opportunities. Five years in the same position without an opportunity to try something new is the general litmus test for when it's time to start thinking about what your next move is.
- **You're just going through the motions.** No job is perfect. There will always be days when you just aren't feeling it. That's to be expected. However, if every day it takes a pep talk to drag yourself into the office. If between updating your Facebook friends on what you had for lunch or the ugly sweater your officemate is wearing you only manage to eke out a couple of e-mails before calling it a day, it's safe to say it's time to go.
- **Your heart is somewhere else and you have the means or the right opportunity to pursue that calling.** If you have a desire that keeps gnawing at you and won't go away that's a sure sign that you need to pursue that yearning.

The key to leaving is to do it for the right reasons and to have a plan. Ask yourself these four questions to determine your readiness to leave:

- Is your decision-making being driven by emotions or have you carefully weighed the pros and cons of your decision?
- Can you afford to leave?
- Do you have another opportunity already lined up?
- Have you given the appropriate notice?

NOW, GET TO WORK!

Do this...

- Assess whether or not you are in the right position or environment to accomplish your goals and dreams. If not, have a conversation with your boss maybe there's another opportunity in the organization that's a better fit. No? Get busy working on your exit strategy.
- **Read:** *You Are a Badass* by Jen Sincero
- **Read:** *Expect to Win: 10 Proven Strategies for Thriving in the Workplace'* by Carla Harris

Notes:

Mantra to Master

"Know your worth and your value, and be firm and clear on what that is."

Bethany Yellowtail,
CEO & Designer of B. Yellowtail

RULE #16: GET MONEY

"I like when money makes a difference but don't make you different."
- Drake

When most people think about compensation they merely think of the paycheck that they bring home every two weeks. However, compensation is much more than salary. Benefits and perks typically constitute about 25–33% of your total package. And, the higher you go in an organization, the more of an impact these aspects of your Compensation or Total Rewards will have. For instance, an executive's actual take home pay is often a fraction of the value of her stock options.

Since the benefits and perks a company offers is such a significant portion of your compensation it's important to look beyond the salary to determine the appropriateness of what you're making. Remember, most of the benefits and perks you receive such as medical insurance, life insurance and training are not taxed. As such, an offer with great benefits and an average income may actually be better than one with significant take home pay but lousy benefits.

When organizations determine their compensation and rewards program the goal is generally to create an equitable process for compensating employees. If successful they'll have a well-structured program with a good balance of wages, benefits and rewards allowing them to not only remain competitive in today's labor market but also agile to ensure flexibility and sustainability down the road.

When do organizations make decisions around pay?

- Hiring a new employee
- When an existing employee is due for an increase
- When an existing employee is moving into a new role due to a promotion and on occasion a stretch assignment or lateral move
- When a high potential or "unicorn" employee is considering leaving because of compensation
- Market conditions dictate a need to review salary
- An employee has a scarce skill that is in high demand

Compensation includes:

1. Direct financial compensation: includes wages, salaries, bonuses and commissions provided at regular and consistent intervals
2. Indirect financial compensation: includes all financial rewards that are not included in direct compensation and understood to form part of the social contract between the employer and employee such as benefits, time off, retirement plans, tuition reimbursement and employee services
3. Non-financial compensation referring to things such as career development and advancement opportunities, recognition, as well as work environment and conditions.

Whenever you're evaluating an offer be it at the point of hire, a promotion or some other circumstance, it's key to identify the most important elements for your desired compensation package and rank them in order of importance. You also need to do some pre-work to learn what the market suggests someone with your background and experience should earn. This will not only provide you leverage in your negotiation but it will also ensure your expectations are realistic.

NOW, GET TO WORK!

Do this...

- Search online for compensation calculators and figure out how your current compensation aligns with the industry standard.
- More and more companies are creating Total Rewards Statements to their employees can see the total value of their compensation. Find out if your company offers this valuable benefit.
- Do a test run with the Job Evaluation Worksheet and see how your current role stacks up.
- **Read:** *Getting to Yes: Negotiating an Agreement Without Giving In* by Roger Fisher, William Ury, Bruce Patton
- **Read:** *Get Paid What You're Worth: The Expert Negotiators' Guide to Salary and Compensation* by Robin L. Pinkley & Gregory B. Northcraft

Notes:

Life in the
Real World

Job/Promotion Offer Evaluation Worksheet
Use this Job Offer Evaluation Worksheet to assist you in analyzing and negotiating the best offer for you.

Step 1: Offer Comparison

	Dream Job	Market Research	Job Offer
Base salary			
Sign-On Bonus			
401k Match			
Performance Bonus			
Time Off (Sick Leave. Vacation, etc.)			
Insurance costs: medical, dental, etc.			
Relocation assistance			
Flexible schedule			
Remote work/ telecommuting			
Travel			

Step 2: Values Alignment

Rate each of the following values on a scale from "1" to "5" with "5" being a most important work related value to you and "1" being not important. At the end of the list add any additional values that are important to you and rank them, too.

Values	Ranking	Alignment
Achievement		
Adventure		
Altruism		
Balance		
Change & Variety		
Creative Expression		
Expertise		
Financial Gain		
Independence		
Intellectual Challenge		
Lifestyle		
Managing People		
Power & Influence		
Prestige		
Public Contact		
Recognition		
Relationships		
Security		
Other_____		
Other_____		
Other_____		
Other_____		
Other_____		

Step 3: Ask Yourself:

What skills will this opportunity build?

What is the career path for this role and how does it fit with my goals?

What will I be doing during the first three, six, twelve months?

What do I like most about this role?

What do I like least about this role?

How does this role position me for my dream job?

Do my core values align with those of the company?

What is a typical day, week for this position?

How will success be defined in this role?

Notes:

Mantra to Master

"When everything seems to be going against you, remember that the airplane takes off against the wind, not with it."

Henry Ford

RULE #17
ALWAYS, ALWAYS
BELIEVE IN
YOURSELF

"Our deepest fear is not that we are inadequate. Our deepest fear is that we are powerful beyond measure. It is our light, not our darkness, that most frightens us. We ask ourselves, 'Who am I to be brilliant, gorgeous, talented, fabulous?' Actually, who are you not to be?"
- Marianne Williamson

Several months ago, I was talking to one of my coaching clients and he was exceptionally down on himself. He didn't have one good word to say about anything he had to offer to his company. It was beyond depressing. Finally, in the middle of his mini-dissertation on why he sucked and everyone else he knew was superior, I stopped him. I said "Let me ask you one question. Even on a bad day, do you think when LeBron James gets ready to take the court he tells himself he's just okay? Or do you think he reminds himself that he's a freaking MVP?"

He smiled at me sheepishly. He got my point. I hope you do, too.

Work can be a grind. And then there are those times when it's ridiculously hard. The last thing you need in those moments is to throw yourself a pity party. There will be plenty of people more than willing to line up and pile on you. Don't be one of them.

Remember when I was struggling at the major retailer? The story I was telling myself was only contributing to my downward spiral. What pulled me out of the quicksand I was more than happy to sink into was the awakening I had when I remembered that no one was going to cheer me on, no one would believe in me if I didn't do so first.

Here's the thing. Many high-achieving people suffer from a persistent self-doubt. A constant nagging feeling that you don't belong. In your head, you hear that you're not smart enough, talented enough, deserving enough, you don't have the right experience or pedigree. That coupled with a gnawing fear that it's merely a matter of time before you're "found out" or exposed as not belonging in some way. This phenomenon is known as "Impostor Syndrome."

Even critically acclaimed, award winning author Maya Angelou, "I have written 11 books, but each time I think, 'Uh oh, they're going to find out now. I've run a game on everybody, and they're going to find me out.'"

The library is full of books about successful leaders, entrepreneurs, etc. who have failed. The difference between them and many others is that there was something inside that forced them to keep going and achieve success despite what the internal voice or external critics were saying. With every book, Angelou wrote that voice kept whispering and she continued to write anyway. Rarely was it that great idea that kept them plugging forward despite the odds. No, they were more often propelled forward by believing in themselves; believing they had something to say, something to contribute and by quieting the negative voices that said otherwise and pressing forward. They refused to allow fear to keep them from taking the actions they needed to in order to realize their aspirations. As Keith Harrell says in his book, *Attitude is Everything*, "The loudest and most influential voice you hear is your own inner voice, your self-critic. It can work for you or against you, depending on the messages you allow."

You can't just think good thoughts about yourself, you also have to say good things about yourself. Positive self-talk is more powerful than belief alone. From time to time throughout the day tell yourself something encouraging. "I'm the best at what I do." "I can crunch these numbers faster and more accurately than anyone else this side of the Mississippi." Whatever is going to make you feel powerful. Find the coach that lives within you."

Having great cheerleaders in your corner is important, but no one can do this work for you. You have to believe in yourself. Again, Harrell, "Don't forget, the best coach with the strongest power over your performance is the coach that lives within you."

As Jen Sincero, puts it so eloquently in her critically acclaimed book, *You Are a Badass: How to Stop Doubting Your Greatness and Start Living an Awesome Life*, "Because if you base your self-worth on what everyone else thinks of you, you hand all your power over to other people and become dependent on a source outside of yourself for validation. Then you wind up chasing after something you have no control over, and should that something suddenly place its focus somewhere else, or change its mind and decide you're no longer very interesting, you end up with a full-blown identity crisis."

Mic drop.

NOW, GET TO WORK!

Do this...
- Write down 3 significant accomplishments. Post them in a place where you can refer to them during difficult days.
- Create a personal affirmation/mantra.

Notes:

Mantra to Master

"Today I shall behave, as if this is the day I will be remembered."

Dr. Seuss

HOW TO
WIN
AT WORK

"Instead of wondering when your next vacation is, you ought to set up a life you don't need to escape from."
- **Seth Godin**

Okay there you have it. You may be thinking to yourself, that's a weird place to end. Or asking yourself, how'd she land on 17? Or saying, uh seventeen, did she just run out of gas or have a brain freeze? Really, seventeen? No one stops at seventeen. Don't you just power through and hit twenty.

Nope I didn't hit an interminable wall of writer's block. Or suddenly peter out and throw my hands just before crossing the finish line. So, before roll your eyes and wrinkle your nose at the odd, prime number here's something you should know about seventeen. It's not some boring, inconsequential there's tremendous significance to the magical seventeen. For starters, In the Bible the number 17 symbolizes "overcoming the enemy" and "complete victory." In Numerology, seventeen is responsible for, insight, responsibility, self-discipline, strength, compassion, spiritual consciousness, and wisdom, a desire for peace and love for all of humanity.

Now that we've cleared that up, let's get back to business. Your brain is now officially jam packed with seventeen rules for creating the career of your dreams. Seventeen proven strategies for accelerating your career and getting to the next level, whatever that level is for you. Seventeen proven success strategies that will transform your career from ordinary to extraordinary. Each of these strategies hold something for everyone. Maybe you need to master a few key ones now and focus on the others later. Or maybe you need to create a career boot camp for yourself where you go deep across all 17. Whatever it is that you need you really can't afford to wait another minute. Each of these rules contain truths that, when thoughtfully applied to your career, can have astounding, life altering effects. The kind of effects that will move you from merely idling to making short work of moving up the ladder.

Now, you have a decision to make. You can choose to be like the thousands of people who quit. Those people who decide to throw in the towel and leave. Those people who decide they are no longer willing to play the game or comply with the rules imposed on them by some distant and seemingly disconnected entity, otherwise known as "upper management." Those who would rather leave behind what they perceive as arbitrary, capricious, and unevenly applied rules necessary for organizational success. Instead, they decide they would rather make a go of it on their own. Or, like many others, you have become demoralized but you lack a better option or you fear the unknown so you'll just stay with a company where you are no longer emotionally connected. You will just collect your check, cross your fingers, and hope something changes.

Yep, you can make that decision. Or you can make a different one. With the rules in hand, you can make the same decision that the people made in Po Bronson's *What Should I Do with My Life? The True Story of People Who Answered the Ultimate Question*: "I learned that it was in hard times that people usually changed the course of their life; in good times, they frequently only talked about change. Hard times forced them to overcome the doubts that normally gave them pause. It surprised me how often we hold ourselves back until we have no choice."

You can decide that you will make a go of it. Where others have opted out you will respond to the call. Yes, you can decide to suit up for the game. You can decide you will make it happen.

You may indeed be an intellectual genius, a savant, the next big thing. Or you might be your everyday run of the mill hardworking Joe. No matter who you are there will be days when, despite your many gifts, you will feel like you just don't get it. There will be days, more days than you'd like, when it will feel as if everything around you- your boss, your co-workers, the guy in IT, your vendors, the barista at your favorite coffee shop and maybe even your dog - is conspiring to reinforce that fact.

However, just when you feel like all hope is lost and you're about to throw in the towel, wave the white flag of surrender, or crawl under a rock, you will remember that you know a secret. And, that secret is that even though the rules are illogical and they make absolutely no freaking sense, you understand them. Go figure. And, because you know them, you can leverage that understanding with your own innate brilliance to ensure your success. Lest we forget you are a genius, a savant, the next big thing. You, my friend, are sweet!

Remember the formula:

knowledge, skills and abilities
(you already have or are working on this)

+

the rules
(now you have this)

= **Extraordinary Success!**
(this is waiting for you)

You know those people who always seem to have their own personal map or pre-programmed career GPS? Those people who somehow always make the right turns and who always seem to understand how to maneuver the twisty, turny corporate highways and byways, like they are Mario Andretti on the Autobahn? Those people who have no trouble finding jobs, get promotion after promotion, and are viewed by their colleagues and managers as high performers? Those people who everyone looks at in wonder as if they have some secret insight? Those people who are the envy of everyone else? From the outside looking in, it seems as if they have some mysterious formula for success. "Those people" will be you.

What you'll know that everyone else will be dying to know is that there is no "secret sauce" but there are rules. Rules that determine who will succeed and who will struggle. Let's take one last look at those rules in action...

Mantra to Master

"You don't have a right to the cards you believe you should have been dealt. You have an obligation to play the hell out of the ones you are holding."

Cheryl Strayed

NOW GO.
BE GREAT.

"Don't be good Brooklyn, be great."
- **Jay-Z**

A few years ago, ESPN aired a week-long series commemorating Michael Jordan's 50th birthday. (As someone who played high school basketball in the Chicago area it's hard not to be a Jordan fan.) The series was comprised of interviews with current and former players and coaches, each attempting to articulate what made Jordan, arguably, the Greatest basketball player Of All Time.

As I tuned in, day after day, and listened to Jordan's legend, I began to see how many of the rules were evident even in the career of someone as great as Jordan. What was more gratifying than knowing that even Jordan applied the rules, was that there were many lessons from Jordan's success that could be translated for the rest of us mere mortals and help each of us be more successful in our own right. (Even if we never have a mean jump shot.)

It's not just a folktale passed down from generation to generation; Michael Jordan tried out for the varsity team in high school and wasn't selected. He instead was placed on the JV team. Sad story for a high school kid with varsity dreams. Great news for the rest of us. If greatness was based on genetics alone, Jordan would have been selected for the varsity team, but he wasn't. His game still needed some refinement and that's what he got playing on JV. No one is born into greatness. It's a myth. Let it go. You can make yourself into any number of things, and you can even make yourself great.

Don't just take it from me and Michael. "For almost a generation, psychologists around the world have been engaged in a spirited debate over a question that most of us would consider to have been settled years ago. The question is this: is there such a thing as innate talent? The obvious answer is yes. Not every hockey player born in January ends up playing at the professional level. Only some do - the innately talented ones. Achievement is talent plus preparation. The problem with this view is that the closer psychologists look at the careers of the gifted, the smaller the role innate talent seems to play and the bigger role preparation seems to play," Malcolm Gladwell, *Outliers: The Story of Success.*
See: Rules 3,4 and 13

Michael's career is also a reminder that your mother was right, hard work pays off. So, Michael was relegated to the JV team and used that as motivation to really improve his game. Study after study makes it clear: nobody is great without effort. There's no evidence of high-level performance without experience or practice. Just like when he missed making the varsity team, Jordan spent the offseason getting better. He carried that work ethic with him into the NBA. When he first entered the NBA his jump shot wasn't the best. What did he do? He spent the off-season becoming a better perimeter shooter.

See: Rules 4,12 and 13

There's a great quote from Jordan on failure: "I've missed more than 9000 shots in my career. I've lost almost 300 games. 26 times, I've been trusted to take the game winning shot and missed. I've failed over and over and over again in my life. And that is why I succeed."

A lot of people read this quote from Jordan and focus on the failure. Yep, he failed. Most of us have at some point in life. What's more interesting to me is how he used those failures. Jordan saw those missed shots as data points for getting better. He didn't spend his time in the gym merely shooting basket after basket. Rather, his gym time was much more focused than that. He set goals for how many baskets he would make from a certain spot on the floor and what percentage of time he'd make those baskets, and he continually observed his results and made appropriate adjustments. He did that for hours every day. It's a concept that researchers refer to as deliberate practice. Deliberate practice is doing something with the clear intention to get better at it. It requires setting stretch goals, seeking feedback (yours as well as others) on results, and constant repetition.

You're probably saying, well that's easy for Michael Jordan, he can spend the day shooting 500 baskets. It's much harder to apply those concepts to more intangible things like making judgments and decisions with imperfect information in an uncertain environment, interacting with people, and seeking information. Can you really practice "work?". Yep, you sure can. Ask to be on project teams, volunteer for special assignments, get involved outside of work in professional or nonprofit organizations. Use those experiences to continue to refine (practice) your skills.

See: Rules 1 and 14

Early in his professional career, Michael cemented his greatness as an individual phenom. He consistently won scoring titles, individual accolades, and MVP titles. However, the championship ring he coveted remained elusive until the Bulls made a series of key moves that would set the team on the path to greatness. First, in the '87- '88 draft Chicago took Scottie Pippen and Horace Grant. Two players who, in their own right, would cause frustration to opposing defenses, easing some of the pressure for Jordan to do it all. The next key move was when Jordan decided that to be a true success he needed to be a different kind of leader. He needed to be the kind of leader who could make those around him better. To do this he needed to take on a new role a role that would put him outside of his comfort zone. Michael would move from shooting guard to point guard. This strategic change proved to be pivotal for the Bulls.

Not only did it allow Jordan to elevate his leadership capabilities, it forced him to communicate in a new way and it allowed the players around him to grow into their greatness as well. The final piece of the puzzle was when the Bulls named Phil Jackson as head coach. Though Jackson was groomed under Head Coach Doug Collins, Jackson had a fundamentally different coaching philosophy. Known for his unorthodox coaching techniques, Jackson was able to take the team to a place they had never been, the championship. Jackson's style required Jordan to adjust and even when Jackson advanced a strategy Jordan was unsure of, he went with it because he knew they were focused on the same North Star.

See: Rules 1,7,8,9,10,11 and 12

Jordan's path to success also shows that sometimes rules are meant to be broken. Many teams were confounded by how to stop Jordan until the Detroit Pistons came up with the Jordan Rules. The Jordan Rules were a defensive strategy to limit Jordan's potency. Essentially the Pistons strategy was to rattle Jordan and the Bulls by throwing so many different defenses at them they'd never know what was coming. The thing about the Jordan Rules was that they worked until they didn't. Jordan's tenacity as a competitor and Jackson's prowess as a defensive-minded coach made it only a matter of time before they dissected the Jordan Rules and rendered them ineffective.

See: Rule 2,6,14 and 15

Remember when a few of the NBA veterans devised a strategy to freeze Jordan out in his first all-star game? He made them pay for it during the remainder of the regular season. Remember, when they said Michael couldn't shoot? He went on to win 10 scoring titles. Remember when they said Jordan couldn't play defense? He proceeded to win nine All-Defensive First Team honors and three steals titles. Remember when Jordan beat the Jazz in the NBA Finals while suffering from the flu? Remember that time Jordan retired for a year at the beginning of the '93 season to follow his dream of playing professional baseball? He came back in '95 and won three more championships after an almost two-year hiatus. Yeah, remember that.

See: Rules 1,9,13,15 and 16

Then there are the Gatorade Be Like Mike and the Nike Mars Blackmon commercials. The shot over Craig Ehlo to eliminate the favored Cavaliers from the playoffs, the perfecting of the fade away jumper, the taunting finger wag to Dikembe Mutombo, and, of course the infamous tongue.

Once Jordan proved his greatness the sky was the limit to the types of opportunities that were available to him. In addition, his skill at knowing what he was really great at allowed him to continually create legendary moments that set him apart from other players.

See: Rules 1 and 3

So, the next time you're wondering if you've got what it takes or if the rules will work, think about Jordan. And rather than deciding to be good enough...go be great.

BUZZ WORDS

A

Action Item
Something that needs to either be done or at least placed in a list of things in need of doing.

Alignment
To adjust or make changes. To get on the same page.

B

Benchmark
A standard used for comparison.

Best practice
The winning strategies, approaches, and processes that produce superior performance in an organization.

Big picture
Focus your efforts on the important, overall goal.

Blind side
Catch unaware, especially with harmful consequences.

Blip on the radar
Not important.

Bottom line
The net profit or loss of a company at any given time.

Budget
A numerical summary of an organization's available resources and how those resources are to be allocated based on anticipated future expenditures

Buy-in
Getting approval.

C

Change management
The systematic approach and application of knowledge, tools, and resources to deal with change.

Corporate culture
The beliefs, values, and practices adopted by an organization that directly influence employee conduct and behavior.

Cross-functional
An activity, system, or team that contains more than one functional area within an organization and may involve balancing conflicting objectives.

D

Deliverables
What you expect to achieve from a piece of work i.e. targets/objectives.

Deploy
To distribute systematically or strategically.

Disconnect
A misunderstanding.

Documentation

The act or process of
substantiating by recording
actions and/or decisions.

Download
A briefing based on requested
information.

E
Empower
To provide individuals and or
groups with skills, information,
authority and resources in order
to carry out their responsibilities.

Environment
Where an organization operates.

F
Facilitate
To assist in accomplishing
objectives such as a group
discussion on a particular topic
or in a training context.

Fast track
Place at the top of the priorities
list.

Feedback
Positive or negative information
provided to an individual in the
form of advice on a project or
coaching or counseling regarding
his or her performance or
behavior.

G
Game plan
Strategy for how you will
accomplish a task, goal, project,
etc.; means of operating.

Heads-up
Provide warning regarding
something that will happen.

High-level

Strategic overview of the most
important components of a
situation, project, or task.

I
In the loop
Informed.

Infrastructure
The basic structure or features of
a system or organization.

L
Leverage
Using given resources in such a
way that the potential positive
outcome is magnified.

M
Mindset
A particular point of view,
through which one experiences
reality.

Move forward
Keep on track and let nothing get
in the way of objectives.

O
Offline
To discuss something in a place
or at a time other than the one
you currently find yourself in.

On the same page
In agreement; holding the same
information.

Opportunity
A possibility due to a favorable
combination of circumstances.
Also, a politer word for
"weakness."

Out of the loop
Unaware of the topic or decision.

P
Push the envelope
Doing something that has not been done before

R
Raise the bar
Setting a new standard of the highest quality.

Ramp-up
Learn all you can in a short period.

Recognition
An acknowledgement of an employee's exceptional performance or achievements expressed in the form of praise, commendation, or gratitude.

Results-driven
Focused on solutions or outcomes.

Revisit
Look at something again

Risk averse
Not willing to take unnecessary gambles.

Rollout
The process by which a company introduces a new product or service to different geographical markets or consumer segments

S
Standard operating procedures or SOP
A prescribed written procedure outlining how recurring tasks, duties, and functions are to be performed organization-wide.

Strategic
Highly important to or an integral part of a strategy or plan of action

Synergy
The effect of two or more entities working together to produce an effect that is greater than the sum of the parts.

T
Tactical
Approach taken to achieve a specific objective or to solve a specific problem. (Not strategic.)

Think outside the box
Creating value out of new ideas, new products, new services, or new ways of doing things.

Touch base
Establish communication with someone. Or a one on one meeting

U
Up to speed
Learn everything you can.

V
Value-added
Those activities or steps that add to or change a product or service as it goes through a process.

Vision statement
A statement giving a broad, aspirational image of the future that an organization is aiming to achieve.

ACKNOWLEDGEMENTS

First and foremost, I am over the moon grateful to God for allowing me to realize this long held dream. There is no doubt in my mind that it is and was His unfailing love, grace and mercy that allowed any of this to be possible.

My oldest memories of sitting in my room as a little girl, dreaming of who and what I was going to be when «I grew up», always revolved around writing. As a little girl, I was super introverted and found my peace and happiness between the covers of books. I would devour books. If you found me, you found a book with me or in the vicinity. Every time I read a book without fail, I would dream of people reading the books I would one day write. So now to be sitting here on the cusp of finishing my second book is pretty amazing.

As with most things in life nothing just happens and writing this book is no different. So many people were instrumental in making this a reality. Thank you to the many writers who have inspired me over my life and always made me believe that the writing life was a worthy life and a life meant for me. Writers like Toni Morrison, Alice Walker, Terry McMillian, Walter Mosley, Rosa Guy, WEB DuBois, Judy Blume, Beverly Cleary and so many, many more. While it was fiction writers who transported me to worlds I'd never realized existed and awakened my passion for words, I have to give thanks to the writers of all the non-fiction business, success and self-help help books that helped me see that as great as those books were there was a void and I should carve out a space for my voice. I've created a list of some of the best. You'll find my recommended reads later in the book.

I also have to thank Don Hosea, Andre Joyner and Alan Nevel. All three are featured in the book, but more importantly, they've all been instrumental in my success, by offering friendship, encouragement and role modeling what it looks like to be great.

My editor, Dionna Carter. It's amazing how life works. I had the benefit of hiring Dionna to intern for me one Summer. She was a superstar then and very talented, but it never dawned on me that when it was time to make my dream a reality she would have a hand in it. Dionna's feedback and editing have made my writing crisper and constantly challenged me to make this book better. Her insights helped me create more aha moments and hopefully made the final product more inspiring and transformational for everyone who reads it.

My mother, who I affectionately refer to as St. Karene, my sister Chanel and my Aunt Susan who read, re-read and read some more version after version. I'm grateful for their feedback, thoughts and guidance. As well as my dear friend and constant cheerleader, Vonnie. Trust me everyone needs a Vonnie in their life, someone who always believes you can do anything. Especially in those moments when you aren't so sure yourself.

I've had amazing bosses and mentors throughout my life who believed in me and gave me opportunities when they didn't have to. They always made me work really hard (smile), but they always had an unwavering faith in me and ensured opportunities existed for me to continue to grow, develop and move in the directions of my dreams. A few of those people include: Larry & Donna James, Rocky Felice, Shereen Solaiman, Jane Ramsey, Keith Sanders and June Stewart.

I am so grateful to everyone who bought the first edition. Your faith, encouraging Instagram posts, tweets and texts inspired me to give it another go. Hopefully you'll find your feedback all throughout this new edition. I'm also immensely grateful to everyone who will find me through this new edition. My hope, more than anything, is that by reading this book you will have some epiphany, some awakening to finally access all your hopes and dreams.

As I said in my dedication, my two beautiful children have been my inspiration from the day they were born. Whenever writing got tough and I wanted to throw in the towel. Or when I questioned whether or not I truly had something to say that others needed to hear. I would look at them and think about the kind of world I wanted them to exist in. That desire would always propel me on. I hope this serves as a reminder to them that they can do whatever they aspire to and that they should always, always, always believe in themselves.

NOTES

1. Bedington, T, Tarant, S. & Adams, B (2005). *Realizing the Full Potential of Rising Talent (Volume I) A Quantitative Analysis of the Identification and Development of High-Potential Employees.* Washington, DC: Corporate Leadership Council.

2. Bedington, T, Tarant, S. & Adams, B (2005). *Realizing the Full Potential of Rising Talent (Volume II) Strategies for Supporting the Development of High-Potential Employees.* Washington, DC: Corporate Leadership Council.

3. Bolles, R (2005). *What Color is My Parachute? 2005: A Practical Manual for Job-Hunters and Career-Changers.* Berkeley, CA: Ten Speed Press.

4. Carnevale, A. P., & Derochers, D. M. (2003). *Standards for what? The economic root of K-16 reform.* Princeton, NJ: Educational Testing Service.

5. Clark, Dorie. (2013). Reinventing You: Define Your Brand, Imagine Your Future. Boston, MA: Harvard Business Review Press

6. Ciampa, Dan. (2005). *Almost Ready How Leaders Move Up.* Harvard Business Review

7. Gladwell, Malcolm. (2003) *Outliers: The Story of Success.* Boston, MA: Little, Brown and Company

8. Marshall, R & Tucker, M. (1974). *Thinking for a Living: Education and the Wealth of Nations.* New York, NY: Basic Books.

9. Morriss, Anne, Ely, Robin J. Ely,& Frei, Frances X. *(2011) Stop Holding Yourself Back: Five ways people unwittingly sabotage their rise to leadership.* Harvard Business Review

10. Silverstein, M & Fiske, N. (2004). *Trading Up (Revised and Updated): Why Consumers Want New Luxury Goods... And How Companies Create Them.* Boston, MA: Portfolio.

11. Watkins, M (2003). *The First 90 Days: Critical Success Strategies for New Leaders at All Levels*. Boston, MA: Harvard Business School Publishing.

BOOK LOVE

A Whole New Mind: Why Right-Brainers Will Rule the Future by Daniel Pink

The Dip: A Little Book That Teaches You When to Quit (and When to Stick) by Seth Godin

Jesus, Life Coach: Learn from the Best by Laurie Beth Jones

Thinking For A Living: Education And The Wealth Of Nations by Ray Marshall, Marc Tucker

The Power of Choice: Embracing Efficacy To Drive Career Success by Michael C. Hyter

Outliers: The Story of Success by Malcolm Gladwell

The One Thing You Need to Know: ... About Great Managing, Great Leading, and Sustained Individual Success by Marcus Buckingham

The Effective Executive: The Definitive Guide to Getting the Right Things Done by Peter F. Drucker

Being the Boss: The 3 Imperatives for Becoming a Great Leader by Linda A. Hill and Kent L. Lineback

Execution: The Discipline of Getting Things Done by Larry Bossidy

Start With Why: How Great Leaders Inspire Everyone to Take Action by Simon Sinek

The Happiness Advantage: The Seven Principles of
Positive Psychology That Fuel Success and
Performance at Work by Shawn Achor

You Can't Win a Fight with Your Boss: & 55 Other
Rules for Success by Tom Markert

Made in the USA
Columbia, SC
09 March 2019